From a Lump of Coal
To
A Diamond

To Sharon & Bob
We're on the same page
in our life journey
Blessings all ways
♡ A Diamond
8/02/2019

From a Lump of Coal
To
A Diamond

Meditations and Memoirs

by

A Diamond Trammel

Copyright © 2019 A Diamond Trammel

ISBN: 9781076274519

Cover design by our son
Theodore (Ted) Craig Trammel

Ted and Family

Ted and his Family, Deb and Alexander

i

DEDICATION

Still Alive in our Hearts

MOMMA (1944)

Just call her "Mickey", born Catherine Lucille Metz on
October 19th, 1913
to Elizabeth "Lizzie" Steinbank and Fred Metz.
Mickey left the planet on
July 6th, 1991.

This memoir is dedicated to my mother "Mickey" who had the stamina
and strength of an ox and the moral core of an angel. She was loved and
admired by all who knew her. Much of her story is shared as part of my
memoirs within these pages as a tribute to:

A soul who persevered in the face of much adversity
She is the true Diamond

"All that I am or ever hope to be, I owe to my mother."
Abraham Lincoln

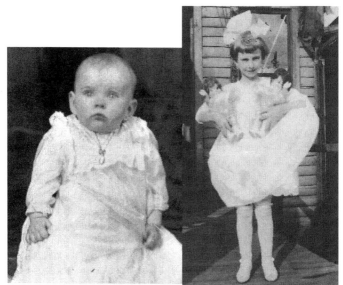

Momma - 1913   **Momma (1918)**

**Momma's Maternal Grandparents
Grandma & Grandpa Steinbank
Center: Momma, Cousins:
Dorothy & Billy Steinbank**

**Momma's Father & Mother
Fred & Lizzie Metz (1910)**

Momma & Daddy (1928)
Mickey Metz & Steve Tamborski

Daddy & Momma (1943)
Steve & Mickey Tamborski

Momma & Bill Rich (1958)
Mom finally found happiness with a man who loved and respected her. Bill died of a heart attack in 1964. He left Momma with financial stability. Thank you, Bill!

Momma & Wally Press
(Paw-Paw Wally)
Retired naval officer. Married in 1969.
Loved life, fishing, traveling &
being with family.

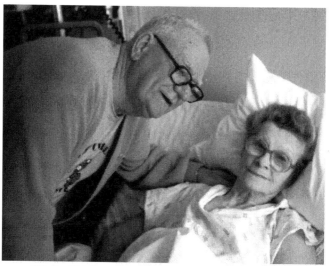

Wally & Momma, her last days ~ July 1991
*She came home to die with her family by her side
An Angel left the earth and it kept on turning.
I couldn't believe it!*

My brother, Rich, and I were by her bedside. I asked "Momma, do you want to go to heaven"? She answered, "Yes." At that very moment, over the television in her living-room where her hospital bed was, the Mormon Tabernacle Choir's voices rang out in glorious praise. It was a truly transfixing moment. Momma closed her eyes and never spoke again. During the early morning hours, with her "Golden Boy", Richard, by her bedside, Momma left the planet.

Watching the Coroner's Office put Momma in a bag and take her body away is a sight I will never be able to erase. I wish I hadn't seen it.

**Poem to honor our
Grandmother on her 75th Birthday
by Sylvia Trammel, 10/9/88**

This special day would be meaningless, if we missed this chance to say, we
love you, Me-Me, you're wonderful
And special in so many ways.
You're never thinking of yourself. You're the gift that keeps on giving.
You gave us life. You give us love.
It's because of you we're living.
You struggled to raise a family. Working hard those many years, to us, you
are the salt of the earth, you suffered and shed many tears.
You've had times of pain and strife,
then all of your children were grown.
You helped each raise a family,
Now count all the seeds you have sown.
You were always there for us grandchildren, by giving advice or lending an
ear.
You touched each one in a different way and
All our memories of you are dear.
Now many of your grandchildren are raising children too, so that makes
you a Great-Grandma,
All sweet "24", we owe to you.
They too will live and grow up under your guidance and care.
When they have children of their own,
Fond memories of you will be shared.
You've created quite an empire, a legacy richer than gold. But the wealth
this family shares isn't the kind that's bought or sold.
Our fortune is the happiness; the love we receive and then pass. The joy
and love this family has known is the kind of wealth that will last.
You're the clan's heart and soul;
The trunk of a mighty tree.
You're the heartbeat of what many call the
BEST FAMILY EVER TO BE.
Today, we honor the lady who's made so many dreams come true.
We are all here to tell you, **Today and always, we love you.**

X

Our youngest daughter Sylvia Trammel (2008)
She has written many poems over the years,
but I think this was her best.

The Whole Clan ~ 1988 ~ Mom's 75th Birthday

ACKNOWLEDGMENTS

Where does one start in thanking those who have made this book possible? There is a huge sense that I have been given the privilege of directing and orchestrating this sacred production of my life. However, I am acutely aware that without having had the right to audition the characters, the entire process is an improvisation. But isn't that what life really is; one big ad-lib?

With an enormous amount of love and gratitude for each one of the players, this drama is presented with much humility. The cast is a vast crowd of heroes and villains, going back some eighty odd years. Each unconsciously played an integral part to help me complete my life journey and can never be sufficiently compensated.

Most especially, I want to ask forgiveness of those who presented me with the biggest challenges and whom at the time, I deemed villains. No one knows better than I, how you were resented and judged, when in fact you were my greatest teachers.

As I list the many names, I am sure to miss a few. Please know, even if not mentioned, that you are carried deep in my unconscious and my heart.

With that said, I thank:
My dearest Mother and Dad, and Grandmother, Liz, the love of my life, Bill, our first born and only son, Ted and his wife, Deb, our precious daughters, Stephanie "Missy" and Sylvia, my siblings, Sis, Dan, Rich, Pat, Steve, Patsy and Clara, all of our nieces and nephews, our grandsons, Brandon, Danielle, Alexander, J'me, Ryan, Fallon and Shane, our grandson's father, Michael, our great-grandsons, James and Jax (until you have your own grandchildren, you will never know the joy you brought to our lives). I thank my many aunts, uncles and cousins, friends, clients:(especially

Kathryn DeSilva and Bea Davis both of you helped me in so many ways, of which only you and I are aware)

I thank my dear soul friend, Alexis Summerfield, who paved the way for my entry into the Metaphysical world, staff members (too many to count), but especially Judi Garcia, Kerry Matthews and Glennie Noste, who were sturdy pillars for The Reunion Center and Pathways Center over these many years.

I especially want to thank those who were directly responsible in helping me get this book to press: Cindy Hrepich, who did the first editing and my angel friend and messenger, Madonna Nichols, who delivered the drafts from Concord, CA to Sacramento, our niece, Lisa Jones, who laboriously used a fine tooth comb to extract the abundance of commas that I sprayed all over this dissertation. LOL! I thank dearest Kathryn DeSilva, who with her expertise corrected my grammar.

I thank, Betty Lue Lieber, who gifted Carol Hansen Grey and I the Reunion Center. Carol was my heaven-sent partner when we assumed the role of coordinators of the Reunion Center of Light and then re-entered my life helping me to present the pictures in this book in a professional manner.

Much thanks and gratitude to Laura Grotz, the woman who brought my book to life with her editing, formatting, technical expertise and marketing know-how.

Thank you to our dear son, **Ted,** whose artistic talent thrilled me when I saw his vision for this book cover, our daughter Sylvia, who honored my precious Mother with the poem on Mom's 75th Birthday.

Thank you to all, without each one of you, my life would have had no meaning. *A Diamond*

Madonna & Cindy (2005)

Diamond and Carol Hansen (1994)

Alexis Sumerfield

*Who knows if I would
have ever entered the
Metaphysical World
without prompting from
Alexis*

Betty Lue Lieber

A Truly Generous Soul

Bea Davis, Bill and me at a Crab feed 2005 ~
Bea's support brought us through the "Lean" years.

Diamond & Kathyrn DeSilva
Sometimes we meet one of our daughter's
from another life and they show up as a client.
Everyone would want someone like Kathryn
on their cheering squad.

FEARLESS 4
Glennie Noste, Judi Garcia,
Me, Kerry Matthews
Throughout the expedition of the
Center, these three have been
the wind in my sails.

FORWARD

Thank you to Carol Hansen Grey for helping me with this forward

I am aware that many authors have a prominent person review their manuscripts and they give a review of the value that is offered by the writings. My preference is to personally inform the reader that my main purpose of this writing is to share the inspiration I have drawn from one my favorite authors, Marianne Williamson. Her message gave me the courage to accept that we are all magnificent beings created in the image and likeness of our Creator.

This famous passage from her book, **A Return to Love** (shown on the following page) is often erroneously attributed to Nelson Mandela. About the mis-attribution Williamson said, "Several years ago, this paragraph from **A Return to Love** began popping up everywhere, attributed to Nelson Mandela's 1994 inaugural address. As honored as I would be had President Mandela quoted my words, indeed he did not. I have no idea where that story came from, but I am gratified that the paragraph has come to mean so much to so many people."

Our Deepest Fear

By Marianne Williamson

Our deepest fear is not that we are inadequate.
Our deepest fear is that we are powerful beyond measure.
It is our light, not our darkness that most frightens us.
We ask ourselves who am I to be brilliant, gorgeous, talented,
fabulous?
Actually, who are you not to be?
You are a child of God.
You're playing small
Does not serve the world.
There's nothing enlightened about shrinking
so that other people won't feel insecure around you.
We are all meant to shine,
as children do.
We were born to make manifest
the glory of God that is within us.
It's not just in some of us;
It's in everyone.
And as we let our own light shine,
we unconsciously give other people permission to do the same.
As we're liberated from our own fear,
Our presence automatically liberates others.
Marianne Williamson
A Return to Love (1992)

Table of Contents

Chapter 1

Guided Meditation: Who Am I?

To prepare yourself for this meditation please read through its entirety. Then sit quietly and pay close attention to your breath. Begin to read again slowly, following the guidance.

How could I have walked so many years and miles of my life without asking this most important question:

Who Am I?

I close my eyes and take three long deep breaths

As I call forth the "I AM" within, I'm consumed with anticipation. How will you appear to me? Will you be projected in my mind as a child or as the adult I am today? Will you/I, be facing me? Will I just see a shadowy, obscure figure that is a figment of my imagination?

With three more long deep breaths, I just sit quietly.

In my mind's eye, you magically jump forth from behind a beautiful silky, white veil. You are laughing profusely. I barely recognize you. You are sooo beautiful; projecting a brilliant light and sparkling with an exuberance that makes my body

1

tingle.

*I have to take three more long deep breaths in order to grasp the
magnificence of what I am seeing.*

You reach out with both hands and invite me to dance with
you.

As we sway, you whisper into my ear and say:

"You will never really know who you are in this life. You are
like an elusive miracle, changing from moment to moment,
as the cells of your body expand and retract and divide. To
define you in one moment is to try to hold you captive and
prevent you from becoming the miracle of the next. You are
in the process of becoming, as all beings are, and will
continue to transform throughout this life.

No one in this present lifetime will ever know who they
really are.

Be content to become.

Just be."

*I take three more long deep breaths and open my eyes,
Content to just be*

Memoir: Who Am I?

"A diamond is a lump of coal that did well under pressure."
(Author unknown)

We were totally exhausted from a long four days seated while listening to the intense sharing of married couples as they relayed their interactions with one another. They were demonstrating how this new technique was helping them come to a better understanding of who they each are.

Periodically, we would break and take time to write love letters to our spouse and then share them hoping the new technique would give us better insight into what our deep dreams and values were, as never before.

This was "Marriage Encounter," which taught a technique in communication for married couples striving to strengthen their marriage commitment.

Marriage Encounter, 1973, provided the forum for my first glimpse of the "lump of coal," my superficial "everything is beautiful mask" was concealing. This new technique had the potential to either solidify and bond the partners or uncover the irreconcilable differences that could save many years of pain and agony for pairs whose marriages would not be able to stand the test of time.

For my husband, Bill, and me it became a tool that we used for several years after, to help us express ourselves in a way that allowed us to be more honest and open. Through this learned process, which included writing love letters, we succeeded in creating a loving environment in which to raise our three children. Our already good marriage benefited to the point that we were able to build a great marriage, though we certainly had our ins and outs, ups and downs in growing together.

Now, with over sixty-four-years of marriage and counting, I believe I can speak for us both in that we are still very much in love and wouldn't have missed this union for the world.

For my brother, Steve and his wife, the weekend opened a can of worms. As I said, Marriage Encounter had the potential to reveal irreconcilable differences and may have saved them ten years of pain and agony if they had futilely tried to stay together.

At first, I felt greatly disappointed and a little guilty since it was I who had suggested they go on the weekend. Eventually, I accepted, according to my brother, "We were in an incompatible relationship."

To backtrack just a little, while much togetherness and joy had blessed us during the first ten years of our marriage: producing three marvelous children, Ted, Stephanie and Sylvia, for us, it was mostly a status quo, day to day norm. We bought a piece of property, built our first home and eventually moved from the Midwest (St. Louis) to Concord, California.

We sort of followed the avenue of least resistance and lived the "June and Ward Cleaver, Leave It to Beaver" kind of lifestyle. Although, this "June" found in the real world it was necessary to have two incomes in order to make it financially. Consequently, Bill and I worked opposite hours, so that one of us was always home with our children.

Those next eight years had passed swiftly, our children grew and I had a nervous breakdown. We survived! I say that casually, not to discount it. This segment of my life will be shared in the Trust and Forgiveness chapters. It was after my "breakdown" that

4

we chose to do Marriage Encounter, a four-day weekend. We had drifted onto a new calm sea and the wind in our sails carried us to uncharted waters with many other crafts with the same destination in mind.

Focusing on our Marriage Encounter experience and the truly fabulous new friends we had made became a huge chapter in our lives. Meeting on a regular basis with these like-minded couples in "circles" and sharing our love letters to our group opened vistas of understanding and insight, enriching our lives immeasurably. We learned to trust our feelings and emotions.

Little did I know that never again would our lives be the same. The social arena that opened to us afforded a whole new dimension of interaction with people other than family. This was a phenomenon not before experienced. However, it was the new self-awareness that allowed me to take a giant leap mentally and emotionally. Finding the courage to be authentically me felt unbelievably light and freeing. A huge burden had been lifted.

Having taken full advantage of the one segment in the Marriage Encounter weekend where you separated from your spouse and spent a full two hours alone in a room writing a letter to ourselves was the "icing on the cake" and the high point of the weekend for me.

Our instructions were to start writing and even if we ran out of new thoughts, just to keep writing and observe what came forth. Trusting them implicitly, I followed their suggestions to the nth degree. The results became one of the many transforming milestones of my life.

Random, pointless writing eventually became auto biographical and carried me to a time in my early teens when I played softball. This was a time when it seemed to me, I was beginning to have some positive feelings about myself as I transformed from adolescence to teen and joined a softball team.

Baseball was a huge part of our family. Steve, my oldest brother, had gone to a minor league training camp with the New York Giants. The St. Louis Cardinal's games were broadcast throughout our home on those hot, humid summer evenings. For me to be assigned as the first baseman on the all-girl team felt like I had "made it."

I loved baseball and softball. As I wrote, it was as if I took on the persona of the softball, a DIRTY WORN softball. I was all right with that! I loved functional, useful, well worn, sturdy anything. A Dirty softball told a story of fun, excitement, people cheering and bats cracking, sending me flying into the air to be caught and embraced in a soft, well-oiled glove. What's not to love about that?

It was only in retrospect, when I began to explore the significance of that symbol being dirty and worn, that I realized this was how I imaged myself. At the core of my being, I felt dirty and worn. I mean, at age thirteen or fourteen and now at age thirty-six no one should feel dirty and worn. Continuing writing, I began to feel tears stinging my cheeks and staining my writing paper. Was this really how I felt at my core? Dirty and worn, OUCH!!

Eventually, my silent tears became a bone- shaking sob. This was a torrential, full-blown, rainstorm that had been held in the dark cloud above my head for many, many years. Not only was I crying for that young child who at that tender age was already learning how to put on a superficial mask to hide her feelings, but

6

by age sixteen years, she was learning how to go over the top and apply make-up, false eyelashes and phony hair-dos to hide how she felt inside.

Pausing to grieve for this child, my impulse was to stop writing. Thinking perhaps this was the purpose of the exercise, to get in touch with old feelings and hurts. It was very painful and I had enough!

It also became clear that my compulsion to always look well groomed, shining clean, smelling fresh and looking bright was the direct consequence of trying to hide how I really felt underneath.

This was a character trait that I felt good about. It seemed others, especially my mother, liked this about me and commented on it on many occasions. Little did they or I understand this fetish. Yes, it was good...or OK, but what was the basis for it? What had driven me to mask how I really felt about myself?

Once I composed myself, choosing to plow on was like it must feel when runners get that second wind and find their stride. Soon the words were flowing again, and the visions became more vivid and clear. Taking on the persona of the softball, I felt instructed to take off the outer cover. Maybe I thought I would refurbish it with fresh, new, shining white leather.

However, my writing seemed to take on a life of its own and in my mind's eye, as I wrote, the ball was being unwrapped. The inner twine began unraveling very quickly until it became exposed and presented me with a small, black ball of coal.

Pondering this tiny bit of black material, I felt distinct disappointment swelling up inside. I had found midway into my thirties that I was allergic to coal. As a child, up until the age of ten years where we lived in an apartment with gas heat, my life was challenged many times with acute asthma and tormenting eczema.

The method for heating our Midwestern homes in my early childhood was with coal burning stoves. I was never tested and therefore suffered not only with asthma attacks, but with extensive bouts of eczema all over my body. At one point, I needed ultraviolet light treatments and hospitalization.

My disappointing lump of coal was almost more than I could bear. What a dirty trick to take me on this journey only to present me with an object so repulsive and harmful. I have an overwhelming sense of empathy for the people in coal mining towns in the Midwest when I hear of their struggles and their losses following a coal mining accident.

For me, the thought of coal mining carries with it unbearable sadness and visions of darkness that are in some way connected to my childhood "night terrors." I have an inner knowing that somewhere on my souls' journey there was a lifetime when this "lump of coal" path, had tragic, life and death consequences.

In that moment while experiencing this utter sadness, to my complete surprise, before my very inner eyes, that "lump of coal" was instantly to be transformed. At first it was like a whisper, then it grew louder and became, not just a suggestion, but instead a booming command.

This was not a voice that could have been recorded or even captured on my auditory nerve or anyone else's. It was clearly and profoundly a firm command, "Break-it open!" In that instance that is exactly what occurred. The tiny black ball of coal, of its own volition, cracked open revealing a solid ball of gold hiding deep within.

Concurrently, the weight of the world fell from my shoulders. The sheer exhilaration that consumed me was as if I had a rebirth. No longer was I the dirty, worn softball that had to hide behind a mask of superficial draping.

Deep long breaths began filling my lungs as had not occurred for many years. I was not just OK, I was magnificent! I truly had worth. My life was not a mistake as I had surmised from some of the data relayed to me regarding my birth. Abortion was supposed to be my fate and comments made surrounding my birth, "It's another damned girl!" were expressed by my father. (This "damned girl" took care of her father for the last thirteen years of his life.)

In that miraculous, instantaneous moment, it was conveyed to me that yes, it is true, "God does not make junk." This was a phrase heard repeatedly during our Marriage Encounter weekend. I understood and believed this on a whole higher vibrational level for the first time. I got it loud and clear! If "I" had worth, then every human being on the planet not only has worth, but they too are pure gold at their core.

All we have to do is help one another find and believe the golden truth. That was a million-dollar moment in time, a two-hour, 120 minute, 7200 second, priceless moment in time for me.

Many people spend years in psychotherapy to uncover a moment like that. Friends have spent countless hours and huge expenses with counselors and therapists trying to discover who they are and what their purpose is. Yes, I would still choose to present myself clean and groomed. However, my new-found motive would be different. I had found the true essence of my being; it was pure gold. Was it painful? Yes! Would I do it again? You bet!

In fact, we did! Two years later Bill and I chose to do an Advanced Marriage Encounter, another four-day weekend. The format was mostly the same, with a much deeper spiritual emphasis. I had taken time off work and was blessed to find time to pursue a three-year Bible Study Course.

This solidified my spiritual path in a way that gave me a new peace and foundation that the eight years of parochial schooling and thousands of daily and Sunday Masses could not compare.

For the first time, I was finding the courage to branch out and experience other denominational ways of celebrating my faith. The churches didn't "fall in", and the world did not end as the nuns had inferred, if I should ever dare to venture from my Catholic origins. (My scary grandmother, Liz, did not even come back to haunt me, which was one of my childhood fears.)

When we heard about the advanced Marriage Encounter weekend, two years after completing the first course, as usual, I was exuberantly excited. Bill, being the wonderful husband that he has always been, wasn't excited, but was willingly there to help me fulfill my dreams and desires. We signed up and my mom came to be with the children and watch our home.

The format was basically the same as our first Marriage Encounter but this time we were with many of our friends from the previous group, and the camaraderie was electric. The speakers were more polished and shared their marital experiences unashamedly in greater depth. Wow! They had really done some heavy-duty major work on honesty and had taken giant steps in

10

their life purpose focusing on where they wanted their partnerships to go.

Initially the advanced course was a little more information than we anticipated. There was more than one set of couples who found sharing their intimate experiences second nature to them. This was a giant leap in some areas for Bill and me. Remember, we were from the Midwest and our experiences were mostly family and church oriented. Pretty puritanical. LOL! For the most part, everything was positive and offered with the best of intentions for challenging us to stretch our relationship. No stone was left un-turned.

Once again, there was a segment for two hours of writing with the same instructions to continue writing even if we ran out of thoughts and ideas. Since my first experience had been so enlightening, though not without challenge, I was anxiously anticipating this time.

Approaching my writing adventure, I remember settling down with prayer and a short meditation before proceeding. Interestingly, I felt as if the well of thoughts had run dry and wasn't sure how to "prime the pump" to get my deep memories stirred and rising to the surface. The bucket of thoughts seemed dry and parched without hydration and moisture. Nothing meaningful floated to the surface.

Repeatedly going back over my first experience became an exercise in futility. Nothing I tried brought about the success for which I was searching. Then suddenly that small little inner voice began asking me questions. "What have you done with your ball of gold since we last met?"

I started listing what had been going on in my life the past

11

two years. Bible Study, new friends listed by name, I had begun teaching CCD (Catholic Doctrine) classes for the church, I was attending charismatic gatherings with people from other churches, etc., etc.

Then came the big question: "With whom have you shared your golden ball story?" That stumped me. The only one I had told was my husband, Bill. I was pretty embarrassed that I had the audacity to claim that I had discovered my core essence was "golden." I mean, how full of pride is that? I could just imagine my brothers laughing me off the planet. I knew my mom would not even be able to grasp what I was trying to say. My sister, who I adored, might think I thought myself better than she.

Truly, I don't know what I thought. It was as if that golden ball message was just for me alone and to be shared only with the one person who knew me better than anyone, my darling Bill.

For some reason this inner voice was urging me to begin to share my story with others. I wasn't sure who would be interested. Once again, my pride and fears were getting in the way. Always afraid that others would think I was bragging or boasting, I kept most of my thoughts and feelings to myself. I preferred to be an observer, a listener, which was totally out of character with my natal horoscope. Often people would comment that they couldn't believe I was a "Leo."

When I learned that Leos were supposed to be leaders and outgoing, I didn't like that about myself. The thought made my skin crawl. In order to become the person that I was encouraged to be felt like I would have to turn myself inside out.

This kind of back and forth banter with my inner voice became more of a mental exercise than a writing one. I wrote some, but the thoughts kept bouncing around in my head and was most unnerving. I was not enjoying this storm of thoughts and didn't even seem to have the capacity to record them with pen and paper.

The inner hurricane was getting the best of me. I wanted it to stop. It was as if I was having a battle of wits with someone I couldn't identify. This was more of an interrogation, demanding I answer questions meant for someone else.

Before I knew it, the time was running out; I was exhausted and felt my time had been wasted. I tried to calm myself with a quiet meditation and deep breathing. With my eyes closed, the golden ball kept materializing and was placed right in front of my "third eye" between my eyebrows.

Eventually, I just surrendered and allowed the ball of gold to just settle in its desired position between my brows. After a few minutes, I noted the ball had cracked and out from within appeared a beautiful, breath-taking diamond. It hovered in front of my third eye for a few seconds and then it disappeared.

I was beyond amazement. Was that really what I saw? Was it really a diamond? At first, I felt overwhelming joy; a feeling of being on top of the world, but then came the self-doubts. "What an over inflated ego I must have." How could anyone conjure up this kind of self-vision?

I felt ashamed and began crying. My throat tightened and I wanted to crawl into a hole. However, my two hours had ended and the bell rang. I wanted to yell, "Wait! I need more time!"

Reluctantly, I went to meet Bill and all I could say was "How was your writing session?" To which he answered, "Are you kidding? I slept!" That's my Bill, simple, uncomplicated, totally honest and doing exactly what he wanted to do. Is it any wonder I love him so?

He is so exactly what this crazy, complicated woman needs to find balance and harmony. By extreme contrast, I had just spent two hours wrestling with who knows what and coming out of that room more confused and full of self-doubt than when I entered.

It was common practice after the MARRIAGE ENCOUNTER. Weekend for one of the presenting team members to host a gathering for all those who attended the session. It was a joyous celebration with delicious snacks, wine and great company. Sharing our experiences with others who had similar insight into the whole process proved invaluable.

Trying to tell family members or friends how great the time was seemed nearly impossible. They really had to have been there to understand the impact those intense four days had on everyone.

Part of the celebration included a time of sharing with the whole group in a wide circle. Once we had been through all the deep sharing from the presenters, our trust level went up beyond measure. Everyone had let their guard down and the stories that were shared were incredible. People dug to the depths of their souls and revealed secrets that had prevented them from being fully honest with their spouses. These revelations touched all of us on a plain most of us had never ventured onto before.

These gatherings solidified our connections to one another as nothing Bill and I had ever witnessed. These friends became our "soul family." Most of us agreed this time together was so precious that we felt the need to continue meeting on a regular

14

basis. Thus, our monthly Marriage Encounter Circles began.

It took me quite some time before I was able to share my "coal to diamond" story, but eventually I found the courage to share it. I was still greatly puzzled by the whole scenario, except that I knew the sense of self-inadequacy had faded greatly. One friend was very intrigued by the story and continued to inquire from me when we would meet, "Have you gotten any more insight as to the significance of the symbols of coal, gold, and diamond?"

To remind you, this was 1975. We had made our original Marriage Encounter in 1973. Two years had lapsed since the beginning of the script. At one point I vaguely remember telling this woman that I believed the significance of my experience was supposed to be revealed to me later, but that I had a suspicion the diamond would somehow be beneficial to Bill and me.

To jump ahead twenty-one years, it took me from 1975 until 1996 to change my name to A Diamond. The journey that Spirit was to take us on was beyond our imagination.

Over the past twenty-one years, I became the coordinator of the Confirmation program at our church. I was given the task to design the program as long as it included certain components of doctrine and ritual. This was a time where I had total dependence on the Holy Spirit's guidance. However, all the self-inadequacies from the past would periodically pop up to haunt me.

Mostly, what I learned about myself was to have the courage to say "yes" when invited to accept a position of leadership. Even though deep within there was a voice that said, "I guess they asked other people and they all said no." Or, "Wow!

15

They had to scrape the bottom of the barrel." I was truly terrified and "prayed without ceasing" as scripture and the nuns had instructed.

On the day that I had a catechism class to teach, I would get up at five am, meditate, exercise to the "I AM affirmations", which I felt were dictated to me by the Holy Spirit:

(I AM Love, Light, Joy, Peace, Patience, etc., etc., all thirty-two of them) and then just trust that I wouldn't look stupid sharing my faith experience.

As the church experience became all-encompassing, I became a Lay Minister, Lector, member of the Parish Council, a member of the St Agnes Church Staff and Youth Minister.

The pastor at the time, Fr. Paul Schmidt, became a sort of mentor in that he seemed to recognize a strength in me that I had never suspected. He truly empowered the "sheep he was entrusted to shepherd." I became one of the "go to" people for what was going on in the parish; anywhere from how to set the alarm in the church to how to run the mimeograph in the church office and loved every minute of it.

My final huge contribution was as coordinator of the 25th Parish Anniversary Celebrations. With the gifts and talents of other parishioners, uncovered within the parish, the church was transformed to look like Noah's Ark on the outside. The great group from the Knights of Columbus prepared a sit-down dinner for 500 people. The next day we celebrated with a full-blown carnival, complete with rides and a barbecue for approximately 1,000 people.

We had anniversary tee-shirts and commemorative wine glasses. To say the least, it was a huge success and was mostly paid for by selling the merchandise, charging for the dinner, carnival rides and food. This may be the venture that allowed me to uncover the leadership qualities on a grand scale that I was supposed to embody as an astrological "Leo." I was literally transformed and almost intoxicated on the high of discovering that true power is in empowering others.

All I had to do was put a notice in the church Sunday Bulletin asking for someone with this or that talent and out of the 1800 families, people came in droves to unselfishly share their gifts, skills and talents; carpenters, artists, musicians, craftsmen, cooks, people with connections to help me acquire promotional merchandise at a discount, etc., etc. I was mesmerized and truly in awe of how the people responded to the needs.

As my "church era" came to an abrupt close (our daughter, Stephanie's stroke) little did I know how this time had transformed me from the shrinking violet into the lion leader I was born to be. I say this without any boasting or sense of pride on my behalf. What I know to be true is that the "hound of heaven", Book: The **Hound of Heaven** by Francis Thompson if we are willing, will lead us down the appropriate path and open doors that we never imagined were available to us. All we have to do is say, "yes."

This was 1991 and I was still going by my birth name, Audrey. The idea of changing my name to A Diamond had not even entered my consciousness. Although, when the thought finally did come to me, I recalled on many occasions, people saying to me "You are such a gem" or "You are such a jewel" or if you can imagine, "You are such a diamond." I mean, really, in all my years prior, never had I heard these statements.

17

Even so, don't we all throw bouquets at one another when something special is achieved? But have you ever called someone "a diamond"? I'm just sayin', I had never heard that expression before, at least not directed toward me.

This is not the place to address our daughter's stroke since that was a huge chunk of learning that I will share in my chapter on "Grief." Suffice it to say, it was this event that propelled me into my career as a massage therapist and the eventual changing of my name.

Unbelievably, upon completing my training as a massage therapist, a Holistic Health Center was literally given to me. The Center was already established and the person running it, Betty Lue Lieber, wanted to open a Center in another state. A mutual friend gave her my name. She called me and offered me the Center, and again, I said "yes." At this stage of my life, I had become totally conditioned to trusting "my life was being orchestrated by a power greater than myself."

Whenever something was presented, I just automatically assumed it was a gift from above. (Unbelievably, I said yes in spite of the fact that we willingly assumed the task of raising our three precious grandsons, ages 18 months, 3-1/2yrs and 10 yrs., since Stephanie's stroke left her quite disabled.)

Viewing the gift of the Center as "heaven sent", when a new friend "divinely appeared", Carol Hansen, and agreed to be my partner, it all seemed too exquisitely coordinated to refuse. Together we set out on a new adventure as the "Parcevals" of the metaphysical world. I kept the Center fires burning, nurturing our staff, and Carol was the greatest of PR Persons in addition to creating a newsletter.

18

To make my looong story shorter, it was in this period, as a massage therapist, that I was, I believe, mystifyingly guided to change my name to A Diamond Trammel, which means "a diamond net." I interpreted this to mean: my main life mission is to gather others and assist them in discovering the diamond within themselves.

While I had received many inner messages to change my name to "Diamond", the self-doubt tormented me until one morning after meditating and while taking my morning walk, I looked up at a real estate sign and the Realtor's last name was Dimond (different spelling). The inner voice I had originally heard on that first Marriage Encounter weekend literally BOOMED, "Today, you will change your name to Diamond!" When I returned home, I shared my experience with Bill and of course he was as accepting as always.

A friend of mine, Alexis Summerfield, who had also had a name change, introduced me to a woman who had helped her make her name transition from Carol Guerrero to her beautiful new name. She advised me to keep the first letter of my birth name, Audrey, to capitalize it without a period, leave a space and then capitalize Diamond. My last name, Trammel, is a kind of fishing net.

Once I could understand the meaning of my new name, it felt more acceptable. Thus, I became A Diamond Trammel, "a diamond net."

My massage training had already been completed and I was now one of the coordinators of "The Reunion Center of Light", a holistic center, which eventually included a non-denominational Sunday service. The people in this new arena of my life were

19

most accepting and comfortable with people changing their given names.

It is recorded in scripture that when a person has a spiritual epiphany, they are often given a new name, i.e., Saul to Paul. **Acts 13:9.** While this was not my understanding at the time of my name change, when someone suggested this scriptural basis, again, this was a large bite to swallow.

My precious mother had already left the planet. There was no doubt in my mind that I would never have done a name change if mom had still been on the earth. She could never have understood. In fact, after completing our Marriage Encounter weekend, and upon realizing what a great friend Mom had become, I wanted to let her know how much I treasured her friendship.

Thinking I was giving her a compliment by telling her how lucky I felt to not only have her as a mother but also as a best friend, my sister later informed me how hurt mom was "that I no longer wanted her to be just my mother, but instead my friend." OMG, had I been so insensitive as to have forgotten that Mom's main life purpose was to be the best mother she could be? The title of "Mother" was her main reason for living! In this lifetime, it was not possible for her to take the giant leap that I was asking her to make. Just because I had found a new awareness, did not mean the other people in my life had, nor could they accept it easily.

So, you see why I say, as long as Mom was on the planet, I would never have become the person I am today. However, I feel sure that in her new heavenly body, she now understands, and it is okay that I transitioned "From a Lump of Coal to A Diamond."

Who would have guessed I would find "A Diamond" hiding in the core of a lump of coal, wrapped in a Dirty Old Softball?

Bill & Audrey (1975)

Confirmation Celebration (1988)

Me, Bishop Cummings & Fr. Paul Schmidt
Youth Ministry Era ~ 1982 – 1988

Building Housing in Mexico

Building housing for the needy in Mexico
This was an ecumenical effort with several other churches in the
area - 1986
This effort is still a part of the Confirmation Program at St. Agnes
Church in Concord CA.

Chapter 2

Guided Meditation: How Did I Become Who

*To prepare yourself for this meditation please read through its
entirety. Then sit quietly and pay close attention to your breath.
Begin to read again slowly, following the guidance.*

*I begin this reflection by closing my eyes, taking three long deep
breaths and allow my awareness to drift slowly into my sacred heart.*

My guidance is to address the many trillions of cells making up
my physical body.

Yes, you my cells have had quite a journey from embryo, fetus to
infant. Then of course on to all the many facets that have
brought me to the being I AM today.

There are so many dimensions of who I have become: spiritual,
mental, emotional and physical.

Yes, I AM truly a miracle.

I take three more long deep breaths, keeping myself centered in my heart.

What a glorious journey this has been, including the hills and
valleys and bumps in the road of my travels.

I ask myself, how many miles of this journey have I spent in a

24

kind of trance or coma?

How far have I traveled oblivious that I had the privilege of plotting my own course?

In my mind's eye, as I gaze around the landscape of my surroundings, I become acutely aware that every choice I have made, every thought I have entertained has brought me to this point on my path.

With three more long deep breaths, I relax into knowing that it was I who charted my journey whether consciously or not.

This awareness is comforting. Even those difficult challenges that threw me off balance and seemed out of my control were orchestrated by my agreements from a past life and had to be experienced in order to bring me to the place I AM today.

It is my choice to either curse those difficult times or to embrace them as learning tools.

Whoa! My Choice!

Where I go from here, is my choice!

Remembering: "The journey of a thousand miles, begins with the first step." **Lao Tzu**

I take three more long deep breaths and call forth my spiritual guides.

I stand between them and hold their hands.

Together, we take the first step.

The I AM that I become from here forward will be

MY CHOICE

I take three long deep breaths and open my eyes.

Memoir: How Did I Become Who I Am?

Maybe it's in my DNA, or a leftover from a past life. My conscious awareness is, as the nuns said: "you are more spirit than human. You are not really of this world, but only in it." This mantra is lived and breathed and permanently embedded in my psyche.

Because of this awareness, I have often been seen as "weird" not only by my siblings, but sometimes by friends and acquaintances. My precious sister once said to me "God! You are just like a nun! LOL!

My early parochial training sank deep into my physical fiber and I learned to pray and connect with my spiritual dimension as though it was an essential nutrient to sustain life.

Does this mean I have always walked a straight path? Not hardly! In fact, as you read my life account, you will discover that my darkest core secrets include "a short fuse" when angered, and my former inability to forgive and to seek revenge which led me down my most narrow, dimly lighted path where I fell into a deep dark hole.

Without making this a litany of confessions, liking to play the casino's slot machines and drinking beer with pizza are just a couple of the many vices that still hold allure for me. Sometimes people on discovering that aspect of my habits have seemed surprised.

Without further ado, let's jump with both feet into the 1970s. For me, this was an exciting time within the organized church. The Ecumenical Council and Charismatic Movement were opening the windows and dispersing the stagnant air that had permeated the stone walls of the religious citadels for centuries.

I, for one, could not get enough of the openness and changes that were transforming the church into a living, breathing entity. While some were dreading the changes, such as the "kiss of peace", I hungered for the close warmth that was being introduced.

Finally! The meaning of love was being demonstrated. Instead of "Jesus is love" just being spoken, it was being brought to life. The humanness of Jesus was exposed and made the mystery of "salvation" so much more believable. The altar had been turned to face the people and we were being exposed to priests that were more real and human. They began to speak in a language we could understand. The Latin language was relegated into obscurity. Hallelujah!

Priests with dynamic charisma were doing a circuit to dispel unfounded fears these changes were generating. Any time a charismatic priest was speaking in our area, you can be sure I was there to listen. It was evident these priests were filled with a new enthusiasm and zest for their vocation. They brought a new dimension of faith and were able to articulate it while touching lives in a way I had never witnessed.

These priests were obviously appointed to help those who were having trouble with the changes. They would make their rounds to the churches and give explanations of why the changes and then expound inspiring insights on the life of the man that this mystery was all about, Jesus.

OMG, I could not believe this was happening. It was as though the hot dry desert was being irrigated with fresh, clean, clear water. And let me tell you, I was parched!

My two favorite priests: Father Hampsh who brought in psychology and psychosomatic knowledge mixed with spirituality, appealed to my love for the sciences. He once shared how he "witnessed a woman crippled with arthritis was transformed before my eyes by the power of forgiveness." And, Father Mangini, who spoke of having a "personal relationship with the Holy Spirit", made Jesus more approachable and human.

They both brought a realness that was relative to everyday life and for me had practical applications which finally made my religion make more sense. Always, they opened my spirit and fed my hungry, childish faith that had almost reached starvation status. In fact, I believe my faith was extremely stunted and had not grown in many years. I was like a child that had been kept indoors away from the sunlight and needed desperately to be exposed to the vitamin "D3" version of faith so necessary for spiritual growth.

These two holy men will never know how their presence caused me to begin to exercise my spiritual muscles. I began devouring books on spiritual development and self-help. My meager library expanded by leaps and bounds. All this new spiritual knowledge caused me to wonder how these gifted men became the people they are. I wanted to say, "Don't just tell me where you are and who you are, tell me how you got there!"

Yes, I wanted to hear their personal stories. What in their childhood helped them make choices that formed them into people of compassion and love and peace and so much more? Who and what events stimulated their spiritual muscles and motivated them to share their spirituality?

I mean, that's what bothered me most about the messages of the goodness of Jesus. Was I supposed to accept that he was "born that way"? I mean really, if he was made of divine stuff, then please, be more patient with us peons who are mere flesh and blood.

It was obvious to me that I wasn't born with the kind of spirituality that allowed me to embody a heart that was full of compassion and love. I had to learn the hard way how to become more loving and caring. Did these inspiring priests have to learn these hard lessons the same way? I wanted them to expound on their spiritual development and not just tell me about someone else's journey.

Their stories were the stuff for which I hungered. This is exactly the kind of thinking that has motivated me to want to write my story. Not that I have achieved the heights to which I aspire. But hopefully, I have evolved to at least a slightly higher vibration than when I came into this earthly realm. Believing it would be incredibly helpful if each person would take the time to share the insights into their own spiritual evolution; perhaps we can help one another grow and evolve to our highest potential. For me that means raising our "vibrational frequency."

Yes, I have had clients in my spiritual counseling sessions, on occasion, who ask me how I came by my beliefs and high ideals. They confided, in so many words: "I recognize in you a spiritual quality I want to know more about." At first, I was more than humbled and even shocked with disbelief by their inquiry.

Eventually, after taking some inventory, it became apparent my spiritual journey had some milestones that were perhaps worthy of sharing and could help others on their trek. Some of my life events may even be beneficial to a person seeking a more personal relationship with their higher self. Hopefully, what I have been inspired to share will satisfy someone else's curiosity if ever asked of me again, "How Did You Become the Person You Are?"

Based on my own spiritual revelations, I sincerely believe each human is at their core, a pure, crystal clear diamond. Over the many years, as I say aloud the affirmations, preceded by "I AM", it is with the firm conviction that we all have these magnificent virtues buried deep inside. Our mission is to go within and allow them to rise to the surface. I once had someone comment on my writings that "they sounded arrogant."

So not to be deterred by this comment, I say, "This is my guidance that I am following." Perhaps this is one of the deadly sins from which I must be purged. So be it! If you find these statements distasteful or presumptuous, try saying them out loud for yourself. I believe it's like pouring water and fertilizer on a seed that is germinating deep within the soil of our souls. It may very well be your own inner child will benefit greatly from hearing what a magnificent being you are.

Following is a list of the affirmations I began saying in 1983, starting with only eight and gradually adding more. Many years later, in 2001, when I opened A Diamond Holistic Massage Institute the classes included exercises with the students saying these statements out loud and sometimes changing them and adding their own. I have gotten feedback from some former students that they still use some of these affirmations to this day. Wow! Very complimentary and rewarding,

30

I AM AFFIRMATIONS

I AM: LOVE, LIGHT, JOY, PEACE, PATIENCE, KINDNESS, FORGIVENESS, HONESTY, HUMILITY, COMPASSION, ENTHUSIASM, VITALITY, UNDERSTANDING, PERFECT HEALTH, BEAUTY, SUCCESS, WISDOM, COURAGE, DISCERNMENT, PROSPERITY, TRUST, LAUGHTER, HEALING HANDS OF LIGHT, SUPER ORGANIZED, VALUABLE KNOWLEDGE, DEEPENED FAITH, HOPE, CREATIVE, GRATEFUL, ESSENCE OF SPIRIT, FREEDOM,

FOREVER YOUNG

Throughout my day, these affirmations are my mantra. It is my firm desire to assimilate these virtues into my DNA. Someone once said to me in a sarcastic tone, "What are you trying to do, become a saint?" I just had to laugh, and respond, *"Don't you know, we are all saints?"* She just rolled her eyes and walked away.

Of course, I'm looney or crazy! That's the label which is fitting for anyone who comes to an awareness of how magnificent humans have been created to become. Jesus himself said, "You will do even greater things than I have done." John, 14:12. I don't think he meant that we had to become fanatically religious. All he wanted us to do is go within and unleash the light of goodness that we would find. "Don't hide your light under a bushel, let it shine for all to see." Matthew 5:15.

I believe that's what Father Hampsh and Father Mangini did. As spokesmen for the new paradigm that was evolving within the organized church, by allowing their own lights to shine,

31

they became the stimulus or activators for others to discover their own inner lights. It was as if we were waiting for permission to dare to recognize and accept our inner power. Even Nelson Mandela, quoting Marianne Williamson, used a similar quote, "It's not that you are afraid you are not enough, but that you are afraid you are too much."

It was during this time of transition that I risked going into other realms of spirituality through the Charismatic Movement. The term "Born Again" was popular at that time and referred to someone who had been awakened to the spiritual dimension of their being.

Personally, it was a term that I preferred not to use. But I heard it often as I attended several different prayer groups. My most memorable prayer group experience came among fellow believers who were very demonstrative in their worshiping. They were totally uninhibited, which seemed *too much for me*. My religious formation came from a more reserved manner. Some of the people spoke in what they called "tongues." All of this was new to me and I remember having doubts about what they were demonstrating being authentic.

As this prayer meeting progressed, I began a kind of inner monologue in my prayers and inquired, *"Are they for real?"* Almost feeling smug and insinuating to my own spirit that what I was seeing was a little *over the top*. I couldn't believe they were really having some kind of a spiritual experience.

Suddenly, for the first time, the voice I was supposedly directing my inquiries to spoke back to me and said, "Try it! Put up your hands and see for yourself." I was shocked! My reaction was almost, *are you kidding? Good Catholics don't act that way!* After a

32

few moments of arguing and wrestling with that inner voice, I soon recognized my resistance was indignant and judgmental. Eventually, my demeanor softened and I relented.

Summoning all the courage my spirit could muster, I began raising my hands above my head as I had witnessed the others doing. We were singing and swaying our bodies as well. After a short time, my heart swelled in my chest and I burst into tears and began crying uncontrollably. Immediately, the person next to me cradled me in their arms and held me as I sobbed with abandon.

Surrendering to my inner voice for the first time in that moment became the most freeing act I may have ever performed up to that point. It was as if a wall had been broken through and a new soft light began shining within me. That was the moment when I understood what it meant to have a *personal relationship with Jesus*. I felt the person who was holding me close to their heart was Jesus himself. *Being unconditionally loved* took on a new meaning.

From that instant on, there was definitely a new something that had begun growing within me. It was more than just an inside change. I was renewed within and without. If someone wanted to call it being *reborn*, I didn't care. I didn't need to put a label on it. A new zest for life, a new conscious awareness that life is sacred and I had the privilege of connecting with something beyond what I could know through my senses.

Of course, it had always been there, but now my spirituality became like a brand-new exquisite garment that was priceless and I had discovered it at the rear of a kind of *sacred closet*. When I put it on, it felt so comfortable that I never wanted to take it off or venture anywhere without it. My new frock was invisible to everyone else, but to me it provided the comfort a baby must get by being swaddled by its mother.

That morning when I awakened, there was no indication that this was to be such a special day. The children went off to school, dishes had to be done, beds made, dinner prepared and then when I kissed my darling Bill goodbye, all was just as normal as expected.

When I walked back into our home's front door after that monumental prayer meeting, I was a totally different person. I had found or stumbled onto that personal relationship with my Master Teacher, Jesus. Words from the song "Something's in the Air Tonight" always reminds me of that sacred night when I entered a new dimension of my own spirituality.

His presence became alive within me and his teachings spoke directly to my heart. Finally, I understood the meaning of "Jesus is your brother", that Father Mangini often declared. "You will see with new eyes and hear with new ears and come to a new understanding", Matthew 13:16, words Jesus reportedly uttered, were now spoken directly to me. There is no way anyone can relay or convey the kind of feelings that go along with such an experience unless that person has had a similar encounter.

A few years later, when I was privileged to have a spiritual counselor, I shared my transformation experience and my perplexity as to what could have caused such a dramatic instantaneous life change. My wise counselor offered this information:

"When a person feels an inner calling for the first time, and surrenders totally, I believe sometimes a hormone is secreted from the pineal gland that alters one's consciousness and raises the spiritual vibration. This shift in vibration can cause an imbalance in the physical, mental and emotional

34

bodies, which can take some time to readjust. It's as if the spiritual body takes a giant leap that the other aspects of a person's being weren't expecting. Some people call this hormone GRACE"

Now that spiritual counselor was by no means an endocrinologist or probably not even trained in the sciences. But I'm telling you, if ever an explanation hit the bull's eye, that one did!

Many years later, in reading the book "One Spirit Medicine" by Alberto Villoldo, he shares on page 35, "Serotonin is known as the 'feel good' or 'happiness hormone. It is chemically analogous to DMT (dimethyltryptamine). DMT can be synthesized by the pineal gland in the brain. Today, DMT is a doorway for seekers in the Western world who are venturing into spiritual territory that was once the exclusive domain of shamans

Perhaps my experience was "beginners' luck." I stumbled into this spiritual realm totally as a novice. After that event, I truly felt like a new human being or like a stranger had stepped into my skin and set up a permanent residence. For the first time in my life, the warmth of unconditional love filled my human body as if a special serum had been injected into my veins, which my counselor termed "Grace." Perhaps it's the feeling someone who does drugs may get. I knew for sure I would never be the same after that prayer meeting.

As my husband, Bill, and I sat on our bed that evening and I tried to tell him my experience, it was evident there was something lost in-translation. He expressed: "I am happy for you, but I certainly don't understand it." Little did we realize that our whole world would soon be changing as a result of that experience.

This was the time when I finally let go of the burden of my

not being willing and able to forgive. My transformation was so traumatic that within a few weeks I had to be hospitalized with what I call "a nervous breakdown." Not forgiving had left a festering scar that could not just be nonchalantly swished away. I had nurtured and fed "my not forgiving" as though it was a vital organ. This was serious! I needed remedial spiritual heart surgery. The pain of the person I had become sent me into a deep depression. The flood of tears I shed in those "repentant weeks" were necessary to wash away the darkness I had allowed to cloud my soul.

As I took my inner inventory, attitudes and actions that were no longer compatible with the new spiritual garment I had been given had to be discarded. In order for this clothing to fit, the excess baggage of pride, vindictiveness and ego needed to be deliberately uprooted and consciously disposed. This was the beginning of my awakened spiritual journey. My new life needed a foundation that was to be built on truth and trust. This, I believe, allowed me to become,

The Person I AM Today

Diamond (2018)

Above: Our dear friends and neighbors, Edna and Derry Moore with us at Yosemite. They too were going through a spiritual awakening at this time and were a huge support as I went through my spiritual transition

37

Chapter 3

Guided Meditation: Compassion

*To prepare yourself for this meditation please read through its
entirety. Then sit quietly and pay close attention to your breath.
Begin to read again slowly following the guidance.*

Walking with Compassion as my companion makes me conscious
this divine attribute is the source of my own spiritual origins.
This all-consuming awareness prompts me to close my eyes.
*I take three long deep breaths, focusing on how precious life is and I direct my
attention into my Sacred Heart.*
In silence I begin to contemplate the vastness of all that
Compassion encompasses. In my mind's eye, the soft misty
energy of Compassion, in a hue of delicate soft rose pink, drifts
toward me.
It feels as if this energy is flowing into my Sacred Heart through
the secret passageway, directly in alignment and at the back of my
physical heart.
This is the same channel through which I receive unconditional

love flowing from Divine Source.

I pause, taking long deep breaths for a few moments and watch this sweet energy fill my Sacred Heart.

A picture begins to form in my mind's eye of myself following behind another person and telling them I will not judge them ever again. "For lest I walk a mile in their shoes", I cannot know the path nor the journey they have charted.

Dearest Compassion, with you I can overcome the old habits of criticizing, condemning and judging others as well as myself.

You dear Compassion, raise my vibrational frequency and soften my heart so that I am then able to accept another's actions and viewpoints objectively as a silent witness.

With one more long deep breath, I open my eyes.

Taking in all my surroundings, I acknowledge everything I see is sacred and has its own vibration. It is because of your enduring presence that I can say:

I AM Compassion

Memoir: I Am Compassion

Tippy-toeing, this then four-year-old gripped the edge of the cold porcelain sink with her pale white, skinny fingers. Gazing across what seemed to her a very long, shiny, wet expanse, she watched the man she called daddy, sobbing as he stirred the cloudy gray concoction he gripped tightly in his shaking left hand.

Every detail became etched deeply on the clean canvas of her small brain. Oblivious, these would be the first memorable impressions she would recall of this giant of a man she so loved.

This was the exact moment I would awaken from the hazy cloud of infancy, when most events and occurrences had left only their ghostly background strokes preparing me for what would become the painting of my life journey.

Traumatic events have a way of hiding beneath the conscious awareness. Remembering, only asking, *"What are you doing, Daddy"*? The answer he gave will not, and I know there was an answer, rise to the surface of my consciousness so that it can be seen in the light of my daytime sky.

It's as if that answer wants to remain in that place of darkness where shame and sadness live and thrive. I have wrestled with the two demons, trying to coax them to reveal my Daddy's words, but they remain forever buried in the ground of my landscape. My greatest suspicion is that he said, "I am killing myself."

Loud commotion, police, firemen, Daddy taken away, me standing on the periphery as a silent witness, with my parent's bed between my safety and all the chaos. The violent scene, vividly etched, as if by a pallet knife, leaving deep impressions and capturing my psyche, holding it prisoner to forever become the caretaker of Daddy, mentally and spiritually, for the rest of his life.

Daddy had tried to take his life and in doing so had placed the brush in my hand which painted a very dark cloud on my life canvas. Terror gripped and smothered me as he was taken away, fearing he was never coming back.

As a child, not yet knowing how to pray, with only the tools a four-year-old had been given, I grabbed onto silence and it became my dearest friend. Most naturally, I easily transitioned into the designated proverbial position of "the invisible child" as identified in the classic "dysfunctional family," as described by Tom Moon, MFT in **Dysfunctional Family Roles 3. The Lost Child.**

The love I felt for Daddy was deep in the marrow of my bones. Impressions of him coming in very late at night and placing his coat over me as I slept in my crib to protect me from the cold St. Louis winter nights allowed the sweet tenderness, he directed toward me to be felt deep in the crevices of my heart.

I came to treasure the aroma of his coat, stained with the smell of cigars, cigarettes and alcohol as if he was giving me his divine hug. A child can create a fantasy out of the most unbelievable artifacts when they are desperate for their Daddy's love.

Daddy did not die physically that day. However, there was a definite shift in the way we ever after interacted. As the invisible child and the youngest, I watched, observed and learned much from my siblings' errors.

Our father was a hard task master. He had been the product of a verbally and physically abusive father, Bruno Tamborski. Grandfather's, jealous, suspicious nature had been inherited by Daddy. Having adopted his father's disease of alcoholism at a very young age, it was as though Daddy never matured emotionally beyond the age of a teenager. In his frustration, he perpetuated the abuse he grew up with on his own family.

Having a dark side to our nature seems to be part of the human condition. However, for some people it's as though their dark side envelopes them and they are not able to sustain their goodness for any length of time.

This is one of the observations that has explained for me the dichotomy of my father. Born the fifth child in a Polish family of eight, many of the old-world habits and customs were a large part of his makeup. An appreciation for cleanliness, good manners and politeness were many of the traits his family embodied. Daddy displayed these traits when sober and demanded our Mother and we children follow these habits to the strictest rule.

It was this large family and their values which drew our mother to him. Dad's mother, Mary (for me Grandma Tamborski) was loved and admired by all who knew her. In her broken Polish/English, she always welcomed us, her grandchildren, with a loving smile and kiss. It is easy to see her face as it is clearly painted in the clouds of my skyscape with her eyes twinkling and the corners of her mouth upturned. For sure, much of the goodness that my father embodied came from his mother.

Although he had the ability to fix, repair, create beauty and was highly intelligent, he was not able to maintain this stance for long periods of time. I do remember fondly mother and him embracing and kissing on occasions and I treasured those moments beyond measure. As a child attending a movie, whenever there was a love scene or a scene of tenderness, it touched my heart and I felt a moment of pride knowing that my parents knew that kind of love….if only periodically.

That dark side of Daddy got the best of him; over time whittling away at the love he and Mama had for one another. This man, I loved so dearly, seemed to become a pathetic drunk while our mother grew stronger and wiser. Eventually, Mom found the courage to end their twenty-nine-year, abusive marriage.

Without Mom in my Dad's life, little did I realize the ghost of the four-year-old, the silent witness was about to rise from the grave of my landscape with bold strokes, painting strong and tall centurion trees, framing the gateway of my journey.

That old fear revisited and again I felt it mingled with the love for Dad in the marrow of my bones. Would my Dad die without my mother's loving care? I had seen my Uncle Ed, Dad's older brother, who I loved dearly, die from a brutal beating when his life was ended in the streets of St. Louis as a derelict.

At age eleven years, Uncle Ed's disfigured image became etched next to my first memory of Daddy and became the second dark cloud on my life canvas. Uncle Ed was the fun/funny uncle who sang nonsensical rhymes (nicka, nicka hopa tato….) and colored pictures and played games with me. When my siblings asked him if he ever went to church, he would answer "Sure, I go to five O'clock Mass with Father Lubalie" (Of course this was a fictitious priest, and we always laughed.)

Mom and Dad knew how much I loved Uncle Ed and when he was dying, Daddy took me to City Hospital where I viewed the still bloody, beaten body of him in a kind of bed with barred railings. It seemed like a baby bed to me and my heart was broken for him. The image is still vividly etched on my canvas. This man I loved so much died shortly after.

Prayer became my solitude. Those two men who formed the pillars of my world, who played such a vital role in my early childhood formation both became such tragic figures. The dark clouds of their presence and mixed messages of influence made it easy for me to create a kind of reservoir on my life painting, where I would house their spirits and strive to rescue them from their own inner demons. I now know that is where "Audrey, the enabler" was birthed.

It took me many years to come to the realization that the actions of these two men, Daddy and Uncle Ed, were a form of emotional abuse visited on a small child who somehow felt great responsibility for their well-being. Of course, they were oblivious as to how their actions and behaviors affected one so sensitive and fragile. I'm quite sure they had no comprehension of the capacity for love that a young child can embrace.

The strong framing for my picture was heavily coated with the "Gilt", i.e. guilt, the Catholic Nuns provided through their hell, fire and damnation teachings. Convinced it was my life task to pray my favorite men into heaven, I followed the scripture "Pray without ceasing" to the letter. (1 Thessalonians 5:16-18)

The burden being too great for a small child, my nervous

44

system responded with asthmatic attacks and acute bouts of eczema all over my body. The coal burning stove of my early years supplied the allergen needed to complete the pathetic existence sickly Audrey took for granted as her normal lot in life.

Through meditation, counseling and hypnotherapy as an adult, I was finally able to see my childhood situation for the reality it was. I now know both my dad and uncle were suffering from a disease they had inherited, whether through genetics or environmental. This was an illness that was beyond their ability to control without help. My husband, Bill, and I, rescued my dad from dereliction when he was seventy years old.

We brought him from St. Louis, Missouri to California, where we lived and had him admitted to the Veteran's Hospital in Martinez. At that time, his diagnosis was grave and he was expected to live only a short time. The miracle of rest, medicine and knowing he was loved brought him through and he regained his health. My joke with him was, *"You tricked me!"* To our delight, Dad lived another thirteen years in our home.

Daddy mellowed with age, though he never stopped drinking his beer and smoking his cigars and cigarettes. For the most part he was a joy to be around. He became our live-in gardener and maintenance man. There was nothing Dad wouldn't do for Bill and me.

It is my regret that my brothers, Steve and Richard, due to their childhood abuse, were not able to experience the good man our dad eventually became. Though they visited him in our home occasionally, the old wounds visited on our mother and themselves remained a barrier they were not able to overcome. It was heart breaking to hear of the abuse suffered, especially by my

45

oldest brother, Steve.

As a man in his eighties, Steve wept while relaying to me the stories behind the deep scars he had suffered as a very little boy. Sadly, he carried all the emotional, mental and physical baggage to his grave. Ironically, Dad shared very similar stories of beatings he had received from his father.

These wounds had caused Steve to leave home at the early age of fifteen years. One of Mom's aunts, Agnes, Grandma Metz's daughter, took him in. Steve once confessed to me, "My greatest remorse is that the harsh task master that ruled our father and grandfather had often been visited by me on my own children." So sorry, "The apple doesn't fall far from the tree."

Steve had become a successful Captain on the Concord, CA Police Department. To look at this jovial, handsome giant of a man, no one would have guessed the scars he was hiding. You never saw him without a smile on his face and his booming laughter delighting your ears.

Many years after Dad passed, while I was in the middle of receiving a therapy designed to release old memories and wounds, the ghost of the four-year-old watching the vision of her Daddy drinking that poisonous potion became vividly visible in my consciousness.

My first inclination was to push it aside, almost arguing with my inner witness that there was no need to visit with such a memory. I had been through it many times and had forgiven all the hurt surrounding the trauma it left me with.

Suddenly, a small quiet voice from within said, "You did not receive the gift!" I felt startled at such a thought and almost said aloud, emphatically, "What Gift?" The small voice whispered

46

as it went on to say, "Compassion! Without that event, you would not have the depth or the measure of compassion you have been given." This was one of the most profound "Aha" moments I can recall.

In that moment, all the fear, all the hurt, all the sadness this tragic scene had caused me melted away. I was made acutely aware that this was one of the virtues I came to earth to embody and that these gifts are acquired at a great price. They don't come easily. This particular event had haunted me for many years and I had spent a great amount of time trying to get the trauma to float to the surface. It had been buried deep in my unconscious. Today, it would be called PTSD (Post Traumatic Stress Disorder).

We are so fortunate to live in an age where we have so many programs and techniques to help us uncover those deepest wounds that cause us to act in ways that don't readily make sense. With the benefit of the program ALANON for adult children of alcoholics, I came to realize that my Dad was the victim of a disease called alcoholism. It not only came to him via his genes, but his father who had the same disease was unmercifully abusive to his sons.

I was told by my aunts that my grandfather was particularly abusive to my Dad. They explained, "Bruno, in his jealousy, accused Grandma of having an affair and thought your Dad was not his child." Ironically, Daddy was more like his father than any of his other children. Daddy once told me that as a teenager he would run away every weekend and then when he came home would sit in the corner of a room and say, "Okay Dad, get your buggy-whip, I'm ready for my beating."

My heart still aches as I recall this sharing. (My Father

shared, "The day came when my Dad started to beat me and I got up and whipped him. He never tried to beat me again." In the era my father was raised, people were not as conscious that this social disease was not something that the victims could just decide to over-come without counseling, prayer and support. Compassion and coming to an understanding of the disease of alcoholism healed many of the wounds of my early years.

It took me over fifty years to recognize and accept the gift of compassion that came to me via an event that I had considered a great offense. I was able to finally say aloud, "Thank you Daddy, you taught me a priceless lesson. You may not have been aware of the gift of compassion you were delivering to me and how many years it would take for me to accept it.

I just want you to know it was more than worth waiting for it to be opened." As I spoke these words to my counselor, I knew my Dad on some level also got the message and he was released from the burden of that event to which he had exposed a four-year-old, highly vulnerable, impressionable child. Daddy and I became one through compassion. I can now say with conviction:

I AM COMPASSION

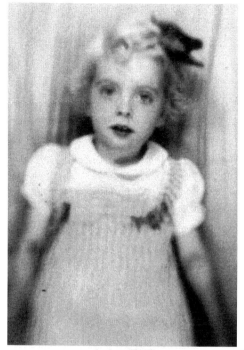

Audrey (1940)

Me, Lil' Audrey, Peanuts

Me & new Puppy "Butch" 1944
Momma & Uncle Ed

Audrey & Uncle Ed
(St. Augustine Church in background)

Uncle Ed loved me & showed it.

50

Daddy & His Mother, Grandma Tamborski
I knew Daddy loved me, but he could never show his love

Grandma & Grandpa Tamborski
Mary & Bruno had 9 children, one died in Poland.
Uncle Paul (died of tuberculosis in 1942), Aunt Raf, Uncle Frank, Uncle Ed, Daddy, Aunt Sylvia, Aunt Helen, Uncle Ted

Chapter 4

Guided Meditation: My Breath

To prepare yourself for this meditation please read through its entirety. Then sit quietly and pay close attention to your breath. Begin to read again slowly following the guidance.

There is a knowing, my most sacred act is being able to breathe and be conscious of my breath.

With my eyes closed, I focus on my Sacred Heart. Gently and lovingly, I breathe the life force of my

I Am Presence into my lungs. It is my first conscious divine hug of the day.

I pause and take three long deep breaths and exhale slowly while consciously focusing on my healthy lungs.

In my mind's eye, I see the flickering flame within my heart expanding and lighting up every cell of my heart. The flame is then duplicated in every cell of my body.

I pause and take three more long deep breaths.

These flames expand until they all become one as a pulsating, warming light. The light bursts forth into my aura and surrounds my entire body until I am totally encapsulated in a cocoon of light.

I pause, consciously breathing my breath of life, sustaining the brilliant light within my Sacred Heart.

A feeling of oneness with all creation begins to fill me with a new appreciation for all that is and ever will be. My every heartbeat reminds me how grateful I am to be able to breathe.

I draw my aura in close as I take one more long deep breath and open my eyes and say

I AM MY BREATH

Memoirs: I Am My Breath

As mother helped me struggle into my heavy fleece-lined snowsuit, I began dreading the cold, knife- sharp, burst of air that would greet my lungs once I walked out into the icy, subzero, morning air. Already anticipating the feel of the frigid doorknob on my small, five-year-old, fragile fingers, I was well aware this long, two-block trek to school would be made alone.

My brothers and sister had departed earlier. We kindergartners weren't required to attend morning Mass at St. Augustine's Parochial School in St. Louis, Missouri and so we arrived at school an hour later.

Only children with debilitating asthma can have any inkling the sharp pain cruel, damp, frigid, subzero air can deliver with every deep breath. Covering my nose and mouth with my thin, tiny hands, sucking the air through my warm fingers, afforded some relief.

Mr. Frostbite soon prompted those small hands be tucked into my pockets to protect them from the ache and tingle I had experienced many times out playing in the snow. If I took short, shallow breaths, the burning was not so bad. Getting to the warmth of the school seemed miles rather than blocks away.

Once in the schoolroom, coughing incessantly and being reprimanded and reminded by Sister Mary Alice, "cover your mouth", can still be heard in the recesses of my brain. Finally, I was sent home (no telephone at our home in those early World War II days). This meant the long two-block trek alone over the terrain I had just traveled. The weight of my snowsuit and the heaviness of the rubber boots challenged my skinny, feverish body and felt like I was encased in heavy armor.

Arriving home, my tear-stained face and runny nose was immediately recognized by mother as she observed my anguish. She quickly removed the encasement of my snowsuit and setup the familiar, makeshift tent, complete with a pot of water placed on a two-burner hot plate.

I reclined without hesitation on the living room couch and felt the nurturing love my mother showered upon me. The warm steam, which filled the confines of the secluded, bed sheet tent, provided comfort and some relief from the pain every breath delivered.

This scenario was repeated over the years with many different settings: in the middle of the night, while out playing, while visiting friends, so many times I cannot recall the number. Remembering, while in the middle of an attack, the fear of the pain and the gasping for breath as I tried to breathe in frozen in my memory like the sharp icicles, I could see hanging off the eaves of our tenement house.

Breathing, the most natural function of a human's existence, is usually taken for granted. Most people, including myself, forget what a gift breath is. We can live for quite some time without food, a few days without water, but only a few minutes without breath.

As I grew in years and moved from the City of St. Louis to the county, our source of heating our home changed from coal (which I later learned caused my allergies) to natural gas. I was no longer plagued with the winter asthma attacks and tormenting

56

bouts of eczema. Interestingly, neither the doctors nor my parents linked the coal to my allergies. They just thought I had outgrown them.

It wasn't until many years later, after moving to California, I discovered how allergic I am to the burning of coal. As an adult, a short time of exposure, when a friend burned coal in her fireplace, rendered me an asthmatic victim, gasping for breath while my eyes reddened and swelled.

Never again would I take breath for granted. I cherish my every breath and know it connects me with this life I so love. For me, every breath is sacred.

You may have noticed that all trainers in meditation techniques begin by instructing their students to pay close attention to their breath before each exercise. The Five-Minute Meditations, which are included preceding my memoirs, all utilize the breath technique.

When I pay attention to my breath, anything that is bothering me is more easily resolved and becomes more acceptable. Upset stomachs, headaches, body aches can often be relieved just by taking long deep, deliberately conscious breaths and exhaling slowly.

In my massage therapy training class, I learned the slower we exhale, the more oxygen we are able to absorb. We also were taught how oxygen is a vital component for digesting our food and in being able to assimilate the nutrients into our body.

Paying attention to my breath seems to allow me to get a better perspective on my life. It grounds me and helps me remember "there is nothing new under the sun" Ecclesiastes 1:9 as shared in scripture and attributed to the great King Solomon.

It reminds me not to take myself too seriously.

As a health consultant and massage teacher, I have instructed my students and clients the importance of breathing deeply. Quite often, I have observed that many people are shallow breathers. While a student in massage school we were taught to remind our clients to take long, slow, deep breaths throughout their therapy session.

Something so easy and natural as breathing is often discredited when you realize that at one time our military folks were instructed to "suck in your stomachs, push out your chest, now breathe!" This is totally contrary to the anatomically correct procedure for breathing.

If you watch a baby breathe, you will see their little tummies are raised with every breath, allowing the full measure of air to enter their body. When a person holds their stomach in and pushes out their chest, they prevent the diaphragm from expanding and are only able to take a much smaller percentage of the available oxygen needed from each inhale.

We can all learn a very important lesson in the technique of breathing, just by observing a sleeping baby. It has been said, "A little child shall lead them." Isaiah 11:6

BREATHE!

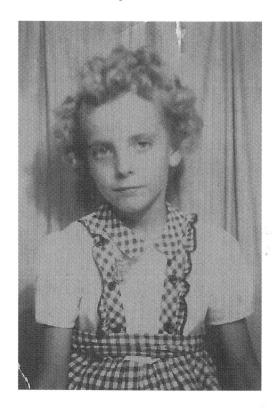

Me, Lil' Audrey
1942

Steve, Richard, Lil' Audrey, Sis
1940
Look at their faces...Can't you just tell they know how much
they are loved by their
Mother?

Chapter 5

Guided Meditation: True Beauty

To prepare yourself for this meditation please read through its entirety. Then sit quietly and pay close attention to your breath. Begin to read again slowly following the guidance.

As I find my quiet place, I close my eyes and focus
on my breathing.
With three long deep breaths, I allow myself to be transported into the center of my heart.
In my mind's eye, I look around my surroundings and find I am in one of my favorite places.
It is very quiet and serene.
I call out "True Beauty, where are you?"
At quite a distance, I see three figures walking towards me.
Noticing the middle figure is lagging behind a few steps, it is difficult to identify them at first.
Sitting down on the beautiful, plush cushion provided,
I take three more long deep breaths and exhale each breath slowly.
The three figures draw near and I recognize Honesty to the left

and Integrity to the right of the lagging figure.

I call out to them, "Hi, have you seen True Beauty"? All three-start laughing. The more they draw near, the easier it is for me to make out their faces. Suddenly, the middle figure catches up and I can see that it is True Beauty. I rush forward and embrace her first, then I hug Honesty and Integrity.

Now all four of us are giggling and excitedly hugging.

Inquiring of True Beauty, I say, "Why were you lagging behind?" She informs me, "It is my nature to follow behind these two close friends. If anyone is unable to recognize them, they won't be able to see me. I am not actually hiding; it is just our way of 'showing up'." I say out loud, "Oh-my-gosh! I am so happy that I learned how to see you, True Beauty." With that awareness,

I take three more long deep breaths

Opening my eyes, I am ready to continue my day always searching for

True Beauty

Memoirs: True Beauty

Dorothy ------? Wish I could remember her last name. In fact, I really thought I would never forget her last name since through her I learned such a monumental lesson. "Beauty is in the eye of the beholder", you hear it said all the time. When my Mom first explained the meaning of that quote to me at age ten years, it still went right over my head.

"You have to come to my house to see my Mom, she is sooo beautiful." Dorothy was not one of my closest friends in the fifth grade when she repeated that sentence on several occasions. I mean, there was Dorothy Dunlap, Vonda Lee Riley, Barbara Ceplica, these were my best friends. They had sort of adopted me immediately when I transferred to St Andrew's School in South St. Louis, Missouri. And we had so much in common.

Dorothy ------, it seems, tried to become one of my very best friends, but I think the other three sort of kept me occupied while on the playground, at recess and even after school as we waited for the school bus.

These are such vivid memories of laughing, singing, dancing and acting out plays in the vestibule of the church until it was time for us to go our separate ways, home. Those times were magical.

Finally, on a day when I had asked permission to go to Dorothy's home, as she had "begged" so many times, I was able to meet her mother. Sweet Dorothy, as my memory now identifies her, took my hand as we walked through the door of her home. It gives me chills to this day recalling the pride this precious girl displayed as she said "Audrey, this is my mommy. Mommy, this is my friend, Audrey." It was as if she had been taught the proper sequence of introductions at this very young age.

I almost fell on the floor! Dorothy had on so many occasions told me, "My mom is sooo beautiful." I think I was expecting "Star Gorgeous"; Dorothy Lamar, Betty Grable, Vivian Lee gorgeous. I mean, this was the year, 1947. Dorothy's mom was in my eyes sort of frumpy and not very pretty. She wasn't even remembered as being very friendly or welcoming. I know, that, I would have remembered. It puzzled me if this "mommy" even had a clue of how much this little girl adored her.

Dorothy, as I remember her, had a smile that would "knock your socks off." Her voice, with its slight lisp, is indelibly stamped on my auditory canal. She was always laughing and had an aura of joy surrounding her. Darn! I wish I had made Dorothy one of my best friends. Her true beauty was drowned out to me by the other three who were also very sweet and nice young ladies.

They were the most popular threesome and were kind to everyone. The entire class looked up to them. I was overjoyed to be their friends. However, my ten-year-old awareness missed the priceless value of Dorothy. I would give "sooo" much to be able to contact her today.

Immediately, when Mom got home from work on that memorable day when I met Dorothy's "mommy", she asked me about my visit. I shared my observations. "Mom, Dorothy told me her mother was sooo beautiful and she isn't. I wonder why she would have said that"? Mom looked at me rather sternly and repeated that well known quote and she added a word and emphasized it, "**True** Beauty is in the eye of the beholder. Dorothy sees her mother's heart. You could not see it."

Then mom asked me, "Do you think I am beautiful?" And I quickly responded, *Mom, you really are beautiful*. Mom burst into laughter and it filled the room. She said, "You think I am beautiful because you see my heart. Most everybody thinks their mother is beautiful." *Really?* Was my response.

Now, I wonder if I was already on my path to becoming a snob. If so, Mom nipped that direction in the bud. How dare I question someone else's vision of beauty? I try to envision Dorothy's mom in my mind's eye. I can see a figure with a dark dress, pleasingly plump and shoulder-length brown hair. But for the life of me, I cannot see the features of her round face.

Yet, Dorothy's beautiful face, long blond hair and huge smile, flashing her white teeth, are available to me as if I had just seen her yesterday instead of seventy some odd years ago.

Sweet Dorothy is a vision of beauty for me. It isn't necessarily her outward beauty that can always recapture my inner sight. It's the magic and true innocence of her being. Her exuberance, vitality and enthusiasm of wanting to share the beauty she found or saw in her mother that always inspires me to look and see True Beauty in others.

I have said it many times and in many different ways in this series of writings: My mother never ceased to amaze me. Her wisdom was so pure and "right on." She saw people's hearts as if by x-ray vision. I recall the nuns saying, "God looks upon our hearts for our motives." How fortunate for me that my mother saw with the eyes of God. She saw True Beauty because she was friends with Honesty and Integrity.

Dorothy and my mother taught me the greatest lesson of all: to look for True Beauty with my heart and not with my eyes.

Our True-Beauty Mother ~ 1944
Her Heart Was More Beautiful
Than Her Sky Blue Eyes

Steve, Sis, Rich, Audrey
1948
We were "The Apple" of our
Mother's Eyes
67

Chapter 6

Guided Meditation: Courage

To prepare yourself for this meditation please read through its entirety. Then sit quietly and pay close attention to your breath. Begin to read again slowly following the guidance.

Today is the first day of the rest of my life. This day I choose to take command of my life as never before.

I pause and take three long, deep breaths, bringing fresh new life into every cell of my body.

I am putting my whole being on alert that never again will I play the role of the victim; believing this is the most sacred act of Courage that can be performed. This day will be walked without fear.

With three long, slow deep breaths, my inner vision embraces my

Sacred Heart.

As I am transported into my Sacred Heart, in my mind's eye, I can see a gentle, warm, waterfall cascading down and washing my body and soul. They are being cleansed of any old fears that have prevented me from embodying the virtue of Courage.

68

With my next deep breath, I pause and watch the warm, gentle, cleansing waters washing away all my fears. I am now totally **free of fear.**

Allowing the moisture to fall on my tongue and tasting the sweetness of the cleansing water, in my mind's eye, an unquenchable thirst is aroused and I gulp the crystal clear liquid into my being until I am totally saturated and satisfied while remembering the **words of Jesus,**

"Out of their bellies will flow fountains of

Living Water." John 7:38

There is an awareness: this Living Water flowing out of my belly will take on the expression of the

New-found Courage.

I begin drinking in full measures of

Courage.

Taking three more breaths of Courage, I begin to bring myself back to present time, acutely aware of the

Fortifying Courage deep within.

There is a knowing that I now have a higher purpose as this vibration of Courage pulsates within.

I am conscious that:

I AM COURAGE

Memoirs: I Am Courage

Excuse me! You tell me what child could ever possibly have a sense of being in command, assertive or courageous when everything they choose to do is monitored and either condoned or denied by all the authority figures in their life? Granted, a child does need some kind of protective advocacy for a time, but stern discipline at too young an age squelches the spirit.

I am acutely aware of the feelings of terror that loomed over me from the beginning. It seemed I was born into a kind of frozen fear, which programmed me to become the submissive, compliant child who displayed no resistance.

On occasion I had overheard conversations between Grandma and Momma about how abusive my Dad had been when she was pregnant with me. For sure, he did not want another child at that time and blamed Momma. That's the reason, I suppose, why Momma and Grandma tried futilely to abort me.

It was as if I was just an observer trying to sort out what kind of existence I had been thrust into at birth. There was an inner knowing that I was not supposed to be here; that my birth was a kind of mistake, a real inconvenience. I mean, how could I have the tenacity not to abort as my Grandmother, Liz, mother's parent, had planned, and worked at so diligently? And then, to add insult to injury, I dared to be a sickly girl instead of a robust boy.

I'm just sayin', if a child is sickly and caught between strict discipline, dysfunction, fear and guilt, you can be sure it is going to take this little person a very, very, long time to have a minute sense of what courage is or have any command over their life.

Watching my heroic, rebellious sister, Sis, only reinforced my own cowardice as I observed her severe punishment each time she allowed her brave spirit to be unleashed. She was at that time the most courageous person I had ever known.

As one of the passive and "aim to please" children, claiming my independence felt like trying to perform a Harry Houdini straight-jacket feat. While these strict limitations were not all from my father and mother, their own unfounded trust, surrendering me to the firm gripping constraints of my maternal grandmother, Liz, and the Catholic Nuns provided the final locking straps.

My parents naively believed the church representatives, as school masters, had all the answers. In addition, out of necessity, placing us children in Grandmother's charge while Mom worked, strict, harsh discipline was the order of the day. Not only was I the invisible child in a highly dysfunctional, alcoholic family, but now I was a charge of the German order of Nuns, "Sisters of Christian Charity.

OMG, can you imagine someone telling a second grader that the Nazis would be coming to hang us from the telephone wires? That our sinful, wasteful ways were deserving of punishment was unbelievably part and parcel of the school curriculum?

We children often heard and believed if God didn't get us, the Nazis were going to get us for sure! This was the early 1940's, World War II era. While the nuns were excellent teachers, they tried to bring us to Christ by scaring the hell out of us.

Talk about creating victim consciousness at an early age, this was it in "spades." Being a quiet child, this reality data was

71

never conveyed to my mother. It was all kept tightly locked deep inside. After all, didn't Grandma Liz say, "You must never bother your mother who is working nights in a defense plant, so you won't go hungry with your problems"?

Guilt, guilt, guilt…. we children were not only responsible for Jesus being crucified, but we were the cause of our dear mother having to work to feed and clothe us. *I am so sorry, what can I do to make things right? All I know how to do is pray.*

Our grandmother, who was supposed to be there to watch over, protect and care for us, reinforced and perpetuated the guilt the nuns heaped on us. We were directly responsible for our mother's exhaustion, according to grandma. This woman we called grandma told my sister and I that because we were "so bad" she was going to come back and haunt us when she died.

Between the guilt and the fear, I, for one, doubted I had any right to live, much less have a say in how my life was to unfold. Vivid in my memory bank are dark nights with lights turned off, (a requirement during 'air raids' preparing for an invasion from the Japanese or Germans) sitting under the kitchen table with my brother Rich and my Sis, listening to scary stories on the radio. The two I most remember are "Inner Sanctum" and "Lights Out." I am quite sure our Mother, who was at work in the defense plant, had no idea the terror I was experiencing, nightly. This was the time our Dad was in the Navy.

However, in spite of all the nightmarish input, I survived, the war came to an end, my Dad came home from the Navy and the Nazis never did come and hang us from the telephone wires. Incidentally, as a child I had "night terrors" and everyone wondered why.

72

Eventually, I did begin to put two and two together and found out who my safe people were, (Mom being number one and my sister, Sis, number two). The nuns became less and less reliable authorities in my life. Nonetheless, I must give credit where it is due; they were responsible for my academic foundation, which has proven invaluable.

Before leaving the topic of the nuns, I am convinced it was their continuous brainwashing: "Catholicism is the one true religion" which caused me to finally rebel and search for the truth. For me, all religions are just a path leading to the same desire for love, peace and harmony. This was discovered early in my teens with a firm commitment to work within the church to somehow devise a way to reform this ludicrous teaching.

I preclude my choosing to finally embody courage with this early childhood account and conditioning by the nuns to demonstrate the monumental task that "little Audrey" faced as I leaped with wild abandon into an arena of "lions" (that's how it seemed to me at the time) to claim my virtue of courage.

The Leap into the Lion's Den:

Ho Hum, some things were so predictable: Saturday nights, lots of company, music, laughter, jokes, an abundance of alcoholic beverages and over- indulgent drinking way into the wee hours. Me, an adolescent, retired to a bedroom, trying to find solace.

Certainly, no amount of sleep could be had, but at least I was away from the chaos. Eventually, the crowd would thin, followed by a semblance of quiet by comparison, beer bottles clanging as they were cleared and thrown into the trash, then interspersed loud talking. Awaiting the inevitable escalation of anger preceding the anticipated explosion, which was as I said, totally predictable!

In the short twelve years of experiencing this almost weekly ritual, Saturday Nights meant tirades fueled by drunkenness and the scary verbal attacks mostly visited upon my mother. My father's jealousy usually implied Mom had made eye contact with one of the men in the gathering or only God knows what other outrageous accusation.

Sometimes Mom was able to divert or de-escalate the barrage of attacks if Dad was so inebriated that he would fall asleep at the kitchen table. Not a pretty sight, but when you are exposed over and over, though the terror was always there, the experience becomes the expected norm and the latter is the lesser of two evils.

Having been conditioned to fearing these explosions, I listened while the abuse was sometimes directed toward my Sis, if not Mom. I learned to become the "invisible child" who was considered meek and quiet. It often puzzled me that Sis chose to be one of the so called "scapegoat children" who seemed fearless.

While not expressing it, my thoughts were, *Please, just be quiet and don't argue with him. There is no way you can come out on top when encountering the irrational ravings of our drunk father.* (Our mother finally sent my precious sister away to a boarding school in Kentucky because she feared our father would kill her.)

On this particular night, the object of Dad's anger was my grandmother, Liz. While at this time Grandma was not living with us, often she would spend weekends with us. She, herself, could hold her own, drink for drink, with Dad.

Everyone else had gone to bed and these two, both inebriated, chose to test wits on a severely cold, Midwestern

January night. I could hear the wind howling and knew the snow was piling, rendering the streets icy and treacherous.

Lying in bed, hoping the encounter would be short lived, I remember hearing Dad say, "Get out! You are not staying here tonight. If you don't get out, I'll throw you out!" My heart became locked in my throat with fear for my Grandmother. Though she was not one of my favorite people, based on past interactions, I knew she could not walk in her high heels the one-half mile to the bus on such a miserable night. (Grandma always wore high heels because she said her arches were too high for regular shoes.)

Where it came from, I am not sure. I jumped out of bed, tore open the bedroom door and confronted the two pathetically drunken figures, now standing toe to toe, exhibiting the bombastic shouting match. I yelled louder than they, "STOP IT! You! Pointing my finger toward my grandmother, go to that room. Dad! Go to bed!"

Meek, quiet "Little Audrey", if I had thought about it, I'm sure I would never have done it. Without a doubt my springing into action was reactive and visceral; certainly nothing planned. In reality, I was terrified of both my father and grandmother. They were fierce, giant figures in my memory bank. Definitely not anyone to cross or confront. *Who was this courageous person in my body? No one I had ever encountered!*

Possibly more amazing was the two giant figures' response. They obeyed like two disobedient children caught with their hands in the cookie jar. They followed the stern directives and escaped to their rooms. I was dumbfounded. Never in my wildest dreams could I have expected their response. It was almost as if they had

75

hoped someone would come forward and deescalate their tirades.

Memories fail me as to how I felt after that encounter. Surely, I was shaking and expecting the worst. Perhaps Dad would tear into my room after me and slap me across the face (which he had done before) for my outburst. I'm sure I was terrified.

It didn't happen. Like I said, for me it was like jumping into the lion's den. I wonder if that's what it felt like when the biblical figure, Daniel, went into his own lion's den.

Holy Cow! Someone listened to me. Later, I can recall feeling empowered. Not at all in a boastful way, but with total amazement. I don't recall neither my Dad nor my grandmother ever addressing the event thereafter, not that night, nor the next morning. It was as though it never happened.

What I do recall is that many years after, my Dad made the comment when Bill and I were planning our wedding, "I hope he knows he has a Tiger by the Tail", while referring to me. Apparently, I may have shown some strong reactions on a few other occasions, though, if I did, they didn't register quite as high on my Richter scale to be held in my memory bank.

For myself, that event did something tremendous to boost my conviction for standing up for the underdog. Many times, over the course of later years, I found the courage to spring forth and defend or try something risky, while always recalling that memorable experience that somehow triggered the hormones or adrenaline that are the necessary foundation for the breath-stealing virtue called courage.

Courage doesn't come easily. Right below the surface of courage, lying in wait, lurks fear and cowardice. Like a glass of cold, icy water smothered by oil on top, the two are so closely connected there is no room for air in between to breathe. Courage catches us off guard most of the time. Occasionally, we may choose courage.

Mostly, I believe courage chooses us.

Daddy & Grandma Liz 1950

Chapter 7

Guided Meditation: Commitment

*To prepare yourself for this meditation please read through its
entirety. Then sit quietly and pay close attention to your breath.
Begin to read again slowly following the guidance.*

A feeling of passion begins to well up in me when I call to mind
those things to which I have chosen to make a long-term
Commitment.

My friend, Dedication, stands before me and affirms my pledge to
keep on keeping on when the going gets rough. She says,
"Remain single minded in regard to those values that hold you
close to your core truth."

I pause and take three long deep breaths and go into my
Sacred Heart.

My inner guides appear and I visualize handing my fears and
doubts over into their care.

With eyes closed and in contemplation, I become totally absorbed
with the sacredness of what it means to make a Commitment.
The awareness that this is a pledge gives me a sense of loyalty and
purpose.

78

Under the watchful eye of my guides, in my mind's eye, I sit quietly beside my friend, Commitment, and realize I am in the presence of my own soul as others look on.

She tells me this sacred vow I have taken, whether with another or myself, says I will honor my word, which becomes a testament to my integrity.

My guides, Faithfulness and Loyalty, shake their heads in agreement, knowing this to be a sacred truth.

I remain silent for several minutes, cherishing her closeness and stroking Commitment's arm as the perception of holiness washes over me and fills me with "Awe and Wonder."

With three more long deep breaths,

I watch as Sacred Commitment flows to the cells of my body.

When I am filled from the tips of my toes to the top of my head, I open my eyes and continue to experience the warmth of this presence in my body.

I now have a knowing, Commitments with myself and others will come easier. I am not alone in learning to keep my word.

My inner guides, Faithfulness and Loyalty, are here to support me and strengthen my relationship with my friend, Dedication.

It gives me a great amount of joy to use the affirmation:

I AM COMMITMENT

Memoir: I Am Commitment

Why in the heck do I feel so anxious about addressing this one topic? How in the world did I ever choose this as an affirmation when I was selecting attributes that I would like to embody? Did I recognize this is, or was, an area where I had a huge shortfall? Certainly, in the past, this was not an area in which I would feel competent to share with authority and conviction.

All I know for sure is that if someone were to observe the events and choices I have made in my life, they could easily conclude that I am a person who fulfills her commitments. Only I know that, while my story may look commendable on paper, the truth may be closer to my having chosen the path of least resistance; the path of least pain. Often choosing the path that would cause the smallest upset for all concerned.

There can be no grandiose feelings of having endured great hardships in order to fulfill my promises. At least not the way I can recall my Mother's example of steadfastness in the face of adversity, regarding her karmic life path, and her marriage. Her courage in staying the course, especially regarding a marriage doomed to failure, would have defeated someone like myself and caused me to run for my life.

Any obstacles that could have prevented my husband and me from achieving our long-term commitment to one another pale in comparison to what I witnessed my precious mother endure to fulfill her commitment to the "sacrament of marriage" as she viewed her vows.

Remembering the anguish, she suffered in terminating their

marriage commitment after twenty-nine years, having a nervous breakdown, still chills me to the bone and is cause for me to want to cry tears of remorse on her behalf.

Mom believed marriage was for life and terminating it was against the "laws of the church" (meaning for her, *against the laws of GOD*). She quit attending church once the priest informed her, she was going to hell as she truthfully replied "Yes" to his inquiry if she was using any kind of birth control. Little did that priest know it was standard practice for many in those days to abort a pregnancy before it got too far along. It makes me wonder which he considered the lesser of two evils.

While I must admit I considered my own marriage vows sacred, no way would that have included enduring emotional, physical and mental abuse in the "commitment mix." So, while I have a good track record regarding endurance and completion of tasks and journeys chosen, my awareness is acute of how far short I fall by comparison to the commitment I saw demonstrated by my dear Mother. Maybe that's why I felt such anxiety in approaching this topic.

Anyway, in choosing this attribute and overcoming my resistance to expound on it, has made me acutely aware this is something I may not fully achieve in this lifetime and I am okay with that. Certainly, I am not inviting situations that will test my dedication to commitment.

AHA! So, there it is, I had to prime the pump and almost admit defeat before I could get in touch with the determination at the core of my reluctance to reveal the failure I had always successfully hidden in this regard. So here it is:

At age fifteen years, I quit school based on a humiliation

and a lie. For years I blamed *this or that* for quitting school at such a young tender age. Anything from my dad's drunkenness to having to work to pay my expenses. Both of which were part of it but not the full true story. I hid it so deep at one point even I forgot the real painfully embarrassing reason.

I still can feel the tears stinging my face and the acute sense of not being able to breathe as I approached the school office on that monumental day. There was a feeling of being trapped and totally alone, thinking there was no one to whom I could truthfully confide my fears. It was a feeling of absolute abandonment and a crushing awareness of all that I was giving up.

I know now that it was my pride that prevented me from sharing my fears with a counselor or someone who cared about my education at the time.

The day started off the same as any other: The long chilling, almost a mile walk to catch the school bus, then the fifteen-minute ride to school, meeting with friends after disembarking and then on to Mr. Wood's science class. I loved school and the whole learning process. Cheerleading for the school basketball team and having so many friends made life exciting and abundantly full.

On this day, (I still remember her name so well) Joan, a classmate that seemed by my standards quite privileged, approached me after lunch. In the course of our conversation asked me, "Who do you think will be voted the most popular for the yearbook when we are seniors?"

This was considered a very coveted honor by all. But even then, I was quite taken off guard. This wasn't even a question I had entertained. I mean, we were only halfway through our second year as sophomores at Mehlville High School.

Why she took this time to broach the subject, unless it was yearbook time and the most popular senior, Jane Eichman, was being honored and it was a hot topic. I'm not sure how I responded, but her next statement threw me a debilitating punch. "I think it will be you." Shocked! Terror gripped me! No way did I want any honor that would expose who I really was. At my core, though I couldn't identify or verbalize it. I was at that time in the deep recesses of my mind that shameful "lump of black coal." Then she asked me the question that delivered the death blow to my school era, "By the way, do you have a lot of those white cotton blouses, or is that the same blouse you wear all the time?"

I immediately lied and said, "Oh, my Mom bought me several of these same white cotton blouses." My face was probably a crimson red and I'm sure I was not fooling her or anyone else. The fact that I did wash the same white cotton blouse on the scrubbing board in the kitchen sink at night and hung it to dry over the heater and quickly ironed it each morning seemed such a small task.

To me, it was totally natural and not something that I thought twice about. Not until I was questioned about it did it become a source of shame. I felt like I was trapped and the blouse was the incriminating evidence that below the surface I was an impostor.

The fact that I didn't live in a real house like my friends at school and my Mom struggled working in a factory to provide food and housing while my Dad drank excessively and paid his bar bill before making sure that we had food and clothing, suddenly seemed like a neon sign flashing off and on to attract attention.

The white cotton blouse became a symbol of the fact that I lived in military converted barracks housing. The car my Dad had wrecked but still drove and had placed a canvas tarp over the back door because we did not have the money to repair it and made him the "laughing stock", etc., etc., etc., all came flashing before me. I wanted to scream and run as far away from the scrutiny I feared. I could hardly get through the rest of the school day. My heart was pounding in my chest and I could barely breathe.

After classes I went to the school office and said, "I am quitting school because my mother is sick and I have to go to work." No one questioned my excuse. No one called my home. No one sent a letter to my family. It was just over, and I was left with a sense of having a double-edged dagger in my heart, relief on one edge and disappointment and sadness on the other.

It was true, my Mom was in fact hospitalized with an acute case of dermatitis all over her body. The doctor had told her that it was good that her nerves chose the route of a skin rash instead of her brain where she could have had a stroke. I did not let Mom know that I had quit school and was going to get a job.

Even the week after Mom came home from the hospital, she did not question the reason I was home during the day. It still blows me away that no one asked me why I quit school.

As I write this, my heart is sad for that fifteen-year-old who on an impulse changed the course of her life, drastically, and no one asked her what her reason was. This seemingly small confrontation with a casual friend became the straw that broke the camel's back. All my fears had rushed to the surface and the burden was more than I could bear.

It makes me wonder how many young people today are faced with life situations that seem overwhelming, with no one to turn to could be helped just by someone paying attention and extending a listening ear.

By this time, 1952, my sister, Sis, had married and moved away. Our brother, Steve, was in the Navy, so it was just my brother, Rich, and me at home. Our father had become beyond intolerable and yet Mom chose to stay with him. She later confided in me, "I made a commitment to stay with your father until all you children were married, and I stuck to it."

Putting this on paper has helped me understand my anxiety and reluctance to address this virtue of commitment. I realize now the monumental pain and shame felt at not completing my schooling was based on pure unadulterated FEAR AND PRIDE.

No matter how much I was committed to any task thereafter, no matter what I completed, this "elephant in the room" of having quit school loomed larger than life and denied me the pleasure and joy of any of my accomplishments.

For years it was a huge source of embarrassment if anyone gave me a compliment. To cite an example a distant cousin of my husband, Jacky, who we began visiting frequently, became an uncomfortable source of emotional pain due to her constantly throwing verbal bouquets my way on every visit. I just didn't know how to respond. A quiet *thank you* and a smile hid the turmoil it set up inside of me.

That inner critic was there ready and willing with *If she really knew who you are, she wouldn't say that.* Consequently, I know my uptightness and vigilantly wanting to achieve and present an "over the top" image gave cause for others to notice and comment. I had unconsciously created a "damned if you do, damned if you don't" inner cycle, which kept me in a state of unrest and embarrassment.

I think I barely breathed just enough to sustain life. In my account of "Who Am I" this revelation may give you a clearer understanding of what a leap it was for me to go "From a Lump Of Coal to A Diamond."

With all this said, to get back to the topic of commitment, I can now acknowledge to myself I am a person who values commitments. Without listing a long litany of accomplishments, suffice it to say at this stage of my life (eighty-one years) I am content that I can stick to the job at hand and complete it because I made a commitment.

I just know that my welfare and best interest are still my priority. I would not keep a commitment that would be detrimental to myself or others. To me, that is just plain "Wisdom." The title of another chapter of my life.

Claiming the virtue of commitment for myself is now possible because my awareness is that my most important commitment is to myself and my well-being.

The fifteen-year-old intuitively recognized she was reaching for a goal that she was not equipped to reach at that time. She did not really fail since she did not have the emotional support needed to achieve it. She did what she had to do in order to survive. I, the adult, eventually learned to quit demeaning her. This young lady loved herself enough to say "uncle" or "enough" and pursued a path that she was able to sustain, which opened doors to learning in the social and business world.

Yes, I can say I AM COMMITMENT and can now

embrace and love the fifteen-year-old inner child who had the courage to cling to her commitment of self-preservation.

Me 15 yrs. and Bill 20 yrs.

1953

The year I quit high school

We were neighbors who didn't know we were committed for life.

As an aside: Bill's Sergeant, commented when Bill was in the Air Force, (his sergeant was also a neighbor of ours) on Bill showing him my picture and stating, "This is the girl I am going marry." His Sergeant, Bob Wickel, replied, "You don't want to marry that girl! She is really sickly; she'll cost you a lot of money!"

Chapter 8

Guided Meditation: Joy

*To prepare yourself for this meditation please read through its
entirety. Then sit quietly and pay close attention to your breath.
Begin to read again slowly following the guidance.*

Believing that Joy is my Divine Birthright, with my eyes closed, I
focus in my mind's eye and take my index finger to begin writing
over and over the word JOY

in huge bold gold letters on the white board within my sacred
heart.

I pause and take three long deep breaths

while sending the essence of

JOY

*coursing through my circulatory system, lighting up the blood supply that
nourishes my entire body.*

Relaxing my neck and shoulders, I am allowing

JOY

to dance through my arteries and veins as the tiny sparks of
golden

JOY

revitalize and fill my entire being with vitality and
enthusiasm for life.

With three more slow deep breaths, I relax my chest cavity.

The sparkling light of

JOY

begins bursting forth into my chest, bathing my lungs and heart
with a feeling of exuberance that sweeps throughout my entire
body, bringing new life and joyous awe and wonder into every cell.

I pause, looking deep inside my body and witness the sparks of

JOY

flowing through my arms and out my fingertips.

With three more long deep breaths, I fan the sparks of

JOY

in my Sacred Heart.

Once again, I follow the sparks as they flow down my legs and
out the tips of my toes. My entire aura is filling with the rhythm
of

JOY

I pause quietly and just enjoy my good fortune, focusing on my
breath

I open my eyes and rejoice, knowing that no matter what
challenges are presented to me, I will choose

JOY

to help me rise above every situation.

Memoir: I Am Joy

If you have ever heard Roger Whitaker or a sweet canary whistling and marveled at the pleasantly captivating notes, you will understand just a little bit why my heart would be filled with joy hearing my adored mother whistling. The notes soared from her as though they came straight from her own heart, tender, soft, crystal clear.

That's what I loved most about Tuesdays; the day after "wash day." That's how Mom ran our household. Mondays were wash day and the day our home would be filled with the aromatic mixture of laundry soap and hearty vegetable soup, followed by Tuesday, the day of ironing

While Mom ironed, she whistled and filled our home with the sweetest comforting sounds imaginable. On hot summer days, with the windows open wide, you could hear Mom's sweet melodies drifting to our ears as we jumped rope or played hopscotch. Nothing filled me with a greater sense of joy than to hear her deep in meditative thought, either whistling or singing. At those times, all was right with the world and peace reigned supreme. The dinner menu for those ironing days was mostly simple. Something like meat loaf that mom could prepare early and put in the oven, smothering the entire entree with onions, carrots and potatoes. The aroma filled our kitchen once again with the joy of her cooking. That's how Mom cooked; one pot meals to nourish her brood of four and anyone else that may happen to drop in. She cooked meals with much tender love and joy and then served them as though it was a special banquet.

Dad's mother, Grandma Tamborski was Mom's inspiration. Grandma, too, always set a beautiful table; napkins to the left of the plate crowned by the fork, knife to the right and the spoon close by (even if it wasn't needed). Each of us children had to take turns setting the table and we all had our assigned seats. Dad was at the head of the table, Mom on his right, the eldest son, Steve, sat facing Dad.

We knew we had better behave properly at the table; one hand in our lap and "no elbows on the table." Always saying please, thank you, yes sir, no sir, yes mam, no mam, pardon me, etc., was the norm. All this was accepted as the only way it was done. People often marveled at our good manners.

In raising our own children and grandchildren, while we eliminated the "sir and mam" rules, we did strive to encourage the good manners. Recently, one of my own grandsons said to me, "Grandma, thank you for correcting us and teaching us good manners. I often have people remark that I am very courteous and mannerly. His great-grandmother, my Mom, would be proud.

Everyone loved my mother and wanted to gather around our table. It wasn't that she was an excellent or outstanding cook. Most of her meals were simple but hearty. It's just that everyone wanted to be around her. She was a great conversationalist and was always asking questions of us children so that we, too, were able to converse.

It was related to me many years later that one of Mom's great-grandchildren inquired of my brother-in-law, Dan, Sis' husband, "What was Me-Me like before her breakdown"? Dan told me he said "So sorry you didn't know her then. She was always laughing and telling jokes. Everyone loved being around her." That was Mom's son-in-law, who she loved and he loved her as though he were her own son.

The personality of Mom is still something that inspires me and fills me with awe. I want to share her with all the world. She was the personification of motherhood and could have served as a role model for all. To me, she was the very essence of goodness.

My aunts on Dad's side often told me how much they loved Mom; citing her joy and laughter were infectious. All this in the face of working in a defense plant as a Rosie the Riveter, juggling the raising of four children on her own while Dad was in the service, contending with a mother who was beyond difficult and then enduring the abuse of a husband when he returned after the war.

If you have read any of the accounts I have shared, of events crowding my early childhood and our family, you must be acutely aware that for mom to be able to soar above the difficult marriage and economic deprivation of the depression era was nothing short of miraculous. Her deep faith was not practiced in a formal setting of the church; however, she did often include in her conversations that prayer was her solace and lifeline.

The many stories Mom relayed to us children as we grew older still leave me spellbound by her resilience. Things like having to borrow $1.98 to buy a pair of shoes so she could apply for a job as a nurse's-aid emptying bedpans. We had only cold running water in the kitchen with, otherwise, outside plumbing. She had us children take turns bathing in a galvanized tub in the kitchen (the youngest child first, me, so the water was cleanest).

The water was heated in a copper boiler in the kitchen to

wash clothes. She and my brothers carried it to the basement where the washing was done on a washboard.

My brothers still recall the time someone dumped a ton of coal *by mistake* at our address (I think it was Uncle Clarence & Aunt Raf Hilton, Dad's Sister and her husband who had it delivered anonymously). Mom, Steve and Rich scrambled to shovel it into the coal chute so we would have coal for the winter before the *mistake* was discovered. My brothers on many occasions would milk the humor of this scenario for all it was worth.

These stories were not shared with us in sadness or as a plea for sympathy or to let us know their hardships, they were shared with laughter in a manner of hard to believe incredulity. I believe it was the way our parents survived the ridiculous elements of what their human condition endured and over which they eventually triumphed.

The stories served me well throughout my life as my own journey's challenges were viewed through a lens that encouraged me to look for the humor of my situations and not take it all too seriously.

After our eldest daughter, Stephanie, had a stroke which left her paralyzed on her left side, we were challenged to help raise her three small children. I distinctly remembered Mom's words as if she were whispering in my ear, "When life gives you lemons, make lemonade." Seeing the compassion and sensitivity that our grandsons embody and express, having lost the mother they once remembered, reminds me that this tragedy served a purpose that we would otherwise never have experienced.

My brother, Steve, once gave Mom a greeting card that on

the front stated, "Mom, thank you for all the years you toiled and labored to raise me" (a picture of a mother washing clothes on a washboard). Upon opening the card, you found the statement "To show my appreciation, Mom, now I'm going to let you toil and labor for yourself." My Mom's laughter, along with Steve's, was uproarious. That's the kind of humor that prevailed in our home. In spite of all the hardships, we laughed at ourselves to keep it all in perspective.

Not being able to afford electricity, Mom had to cook on a camp stove in a small second floor apartment while the summer temperature in Midwestern St. Louis was soaring to 100 degrees. One night the stove caught fire and she had to throw it out the upstairs window to keep our apartment from burning down. She told this story with such bravado that she would have everyone laughing until our sides split. The reenactment of her yelling out the window to the elderly neighbor downstairs, "Watch out, Mrs. Jambroski, I'm throwing the stove out the window." Then Mom would pick up her skirt and mimic Mrs. Jambroski running for her life.

It was a skit worthy of a Carol Burnett, Cid Caesar or Laurel & Hardy episode.

Mom and Dad also shared a story from that time of "no electricity": Dad would hook up a jumper cable to an electric pole at night and take it down in the morning so as not to be discovered by the Electric Company repair men. Aunt Annie Kroger, (an aunt by distant marriage who was not considered to be very bright) heard that we had electricity but didn't pay for it. She called the Electric Co. and said, "I want the same kind of electric plan that Steve Tamborski has." That was the end of our "getting free electricity." We had many a laugh about that episode.

Mom learned to laugh at her difficulties and her admonition is worth repeating, "When life gives you lemons, make lemonade." Both Mom and Dad were great story tellers (Dad only when he was inebriated). I'm sure that may be why all the parties were at our home. Mom loved to entertain. She was often called "Lucy" for her similarity to Lucille Ball.

Even though most relatives had their homes and we never owned a house, they all gathered into our small apartment or rented house. As a child I remember overhearing a neighbor say, "You know those Pollock's, a party every Saturday night" as she rolled her eyes in distaste. At that time, I felt embarrassed and ashamed. While that may not be a justified stereotype for others of Polish descent, from my childhood experience, for our family it held true.

A cherished memory is watching while my Dad and uncles improvised on homemade musical instruments: comb and tissue paper made sounds like a kazoo, pots and pans for drums, two spoons held in one hand and clapped together kept time. No one had an authentic instrument, but the music they made was masterful and full of joy.

My brothers, Steve and Rich, were born comedians and they came by it naturally. They have continued our Mom's legacy of entertaining with their natural sense of humor. Their jokes are quick and impromptu. It was a joy to be at gatherings where my brothers were present. While their humor was often the "Don Rickles" brand (sometimes at another's expense…not my cup of tea), both may have missed their calling as professional entertainers.

They had charismatic personalities, like Mom and Dad that seemed to draw people in. There was a kind of inner light and spark that was undeniable, which must have been inherent in their genes.

Music was always playing in our home. Sunday afternoons with the radio blasting waltzes and polkas or some other contemporary rendition are especially memorable. Mom grabbing one of us and teaching us the Fox-trot, Charleston, Jitterbug, Polka or two-step dances in the kitchen in the middle of her cooking was quite natural. All of us children loved to dance and we fully participated in all the family gatherings. Our cousins were amazed that we all could dance. Even Dad would dance with my sister and me at these gatherings.

While none of us were true song-birds that did not stop any of us from singing at the parties, in the shower or while we were working. Mom sang all the old songs from the twenties, thirties and forties and so did we.

That must be why I love musical movies so much; it seems very right and natural to be singing as we go about our day. Whenever I hear one of the old tunes Mom continually sang, I get a nostalgic vision of her singing while dancing and laughing to her heart's content, filling our home with the joy of her spirit.

Joy seemed to flow from Mom naturally. It was like a continuous well that was primed and pumped by her lilting laughter. Our cousins would comment "I just love Aunt Mickey's laugh. She makes us all laugh." Thank you, Mom, for all the joy you instilled in your children. Without hesitation, I can say joy and laughter are your greatest legacy.

It's amusing to me that our eldest daughter, Stephanie, as a child did not like me to sing while I was doing housework. By the time she was three years old, she would say to me "Don't sing!" It was hilarious for this tiny little blonde imp of a person to speak so authoritatively at such a young age and with such command.

As an aside, my Aunt Rose, on hearing that we named our daughter, Stephanie, exclaimed, "Oh no, she will be so bossy!" She then went on to tell me she had a landlady with the same name, "and boy, was she bossy!" It gave us a good laugh. Our daughter, Stephanie, and I still laugh over this.

It's with much gratitude that I look back at the many dark events of my childhood that my mother made more endurable by her love, joy and zest for life. It is important for me to share the gifts she passed on to us so that our children and grandchildren can know this woman who overcame a childhood of tragedy and chose to rise above her past. She not only rose above, but she infused her life and ours with

JOY

So much joy was also had with our cousins
at picnics. This was at Sylvan Springs in
1947
Left to right
Buddy Tamborski, Wife Mary, Bert, Len Tamborski
Sonny Schlef, Richard Tamborski, Earl Schleff, Me, Annette Kroger

Chapter 9

Guided Meditation: Faithfulness

To prepare yourself for this meditation please read through its entirety. Then sit quietly and pay close attention to your breath. Begin to read again slowly following the guidance.

As I settle down quietly, taking three long deep breaths and closing my eyes,

I pause and get a vision personifying the Virtue Faithfulness.

Heavenly Father, Divine Mother, all the Angels and Saints, as I breathe in the constant flow of the essence of this virtue, my heart feels lighter and relaxation waves over my body.

Beginning at the farthest extremity of my physical body, I instruct my feet to relax and allow faithfulness to penetrate not only my soles, but also the very soul of my existence.

I then begin breathing this virtue up through the core of my being.

I pause taking three more long deep breaths while allowing this essence to fill all my senses.

99

In my mind's eye, I am tasting the sweetness of faithfulness, inhaling its fragrance, hearing its melodic harmony as I feel the vibrations strumming on the strings of my heart.

I am totally saturated with my

Virtue, Faithfulness.

My prayer is that I AM allowed to assimilate this pure goodness into the marrow of my bones so that I can manifest it into all my life decisions and practices.

After three long deep breaths,

I open my eyes and consciously gather faithfulness into my dominant hand and press it into my physical heart with the intention of infusing it into my every heartbeat as I affirm

I AM FAITHFULNESS

Memoir: I Am Faithfulness

Yes, you guessed it! Almost every virtue I hope to embody was somehow inspired by the visual aid of having witnessed it demonstrated by my mother. In my other writings, I have already elaborated and shared her steadfastness and dedication to family and marriage. Having used many other words to describe her ability to fulfill commitments, here I want to honor her unwavering love with the virtue of Faithfulness.

The title of this writing is "I AM Faithfulness." I want to be sure to clarify this is an affirmation that I use daily in the hope that my desire to embody this virtue will continue to cling, even if precariously, to my DNA.

The important aspect for me is that I know it is possible to embody this virtue since I have seen it demonstrated by common, ordinary people, not some predestined avatars. Their faithfulness has inspired me to want to own it for myself.

Think about it! How many people in your life would fit into that category? I myself must admit my own faithful category group is pretty sparse. But I do feel privileged to share that I have known more than a few.

Recently, a profound statement printed by a columnist in our local newspaper struck a chord within me, loud and clear. It still vibrates with a deep knowing and summing up so many of my truths. He stated, "In relationships, there are two kinds of people, 'givers and takers. When two 'takers' get together, it may last a year. With a 'giver' and a 'taker', it can last anywhere from ten to twenty years. Two 'givers' can and usually will create a relationship that has the potential to last a lifetime."

Whoa, that really hit me! Recalling the many matings, anywhere from aunts and uncles to casual colleagues, I have observed over my lifetime, while it may not be a hundred percent....it sure rang pretty true.

God bless my precious mother; at the young age of fourteen years how could she know she was not mating with an equal partner? In spite of the imbalance, she embodied faithfulness for the endurance of their twenty-nine-year marriage.

Mom was a 'giver'. She always "gave people the benefit of the doubt." She was the champion of the underdog and ours was the "go-to house" when there was no other safe place to go. Many times, there were people down on their luck who found refuge on our couch or a pallet on the floor.

We always had room for "one more." Sadly, Mom had partnered with a 'taker'. While Dad was more than generous with his friends, he somehow had never learned to put his family ahead of the crowd. Consequently, it held true, Mom gave one-hundred and twenty-five percent to a man who was only capable of giving fifty percent.

Somewhere, early in their marriage, Mom created a bond with us children that somehow fulfilled her capacity for faithfulness. And so, this gets me back to an event that was overheard by me at age 6 or 7 yrs. old, as mother was relating the following account to a friend. "Yes, it is sometimes hard on Fridays when we are all getting paid and leaving the factory (Mom's Rosie the Riveter phase). The men know our husbands are away in the service and we are lonely. They stand outside and wave their paychecks and invite us women for a night out for a 'good time'. I sometimes feel like crying, but I think about my four kids waiting at home for me and it makes me strong and I can look the other way."

Even as a youngster. I felt the love in mother's words, as at no other time. It placed a big chunk of the diamond I aspired to become into my heart. Knowing at that tender age, my mother would die for me if need be. That made me feel her unconditional love and faithfulness, filling me with renewed life force. Faithfulness became a coveted treasure.

To further share and affirm my conclusions as to mother's goodness, recently Denise Patterson, a dear daughter, of my Aunt Laura, one of mom's oldest lifetime friends (no relation, but we called her aunt), sent me an email and relayed a story her mother had told her many years ago.

"My mom and your mom, as two young ladies, probably in their early twenties, were Nurses-aids and doing the most servile work at the City Hospital. Your mom's beauty and compassion were noticed by a patient. He was the patriarch, Barron Busch, of the notable Anheuser Busch Brewing Corporation. He invited your mom to become his personal aid and to travel with him to Europe. Your mom declined, telling him she had four children, but recommended her friend, my mom, who was single at the time. My mom, who was also a very beautiful woman, was in love with Dad and was afraid he would not wait for her. She too declined the generous offer." My Mom had never shared this story with me.

The rest is history. Yes, Aunt Laura is also on my sparse list under the "faithfulness category." She and Uncle Vic married and stayed together for the remainder of their lives. (Two givers, for sure!)

While I do not claim to be any beauty, there have been a few opportunities to stray from the commitment to my marriage path. After all, when we are working out in the public, we do not wear blinders. Many times, we are spending more time with coworkers than with our chosen lifetime partners.

Mother's example was especially needed by me at a time when I was in the state of "not forgiving" and feeling shaky in regard to faithfulness in my own marriage commitment. Those were years when I licked and nurtured my wounds, held onto not forgiving, feeling betrayed and in my immaturity, wanting to dole out "an eye for an eye"

A very huge factor for me was that our children were my treasures and because of my mother's exemplary modeling and the love she had for her children, I stayed the steady course.

Thank you, Mom, for the lessons and examples you imprinted on my heart. Because of your example, the flame of our marriage love was rekindled, and we have happily stood the test of time.

While my religious upbringing may have had some effect on my decisions to choose faithfulness, the largest chunk was what my mom placed in my heart in those most impressionable years. Today, I can say with much gratitude to you, Mom,

I AM FILLED WITH FAITHFULNESS

Aunt Laura & Uncle Vic (1953)
Mom and Dad's 25th Celebration

Mom & Dad's 25th Anniversary (1953)
Sis, Mom, *(Mom always closed her eyes for camera flashes)* **Rich, Daddy & Me**

105

Chapter 10

Guided Meditation: Modesty

To prepare yourself for this meditation please read through its entirety. Then sit quietly and pay close attention to your breath. Begin to read again slowly following the guidance.

Closing my eyes,
I envision my Sacred Heart opening wide.
I take three long deep breaths.
I deliberately exhale each breath slowly.
Dearest Modesty, please come and sit with me.
In my mind's auditory hearing channel, I can hear the swishing of her skirts as she glides softly and snuggles next to me.
Her response is so very supportive and reassuring that it fills me with awe and wonder.
I must pause and take three more long slow breaths before proceeding.
Modesty speaks softly into my left ear.
"You were born into an age that in many regions does not recognize the value of being modest. Therefore, I have been on a long sabbatical, visiting where I am valued.

Each age of the human evolutionary path has a new set of values.
All are necessary for learning.

I patiently wait until I am called upon to instruct, inspire and become more visible.

The pendulum swings in each direction. Sometimes it may swing too far in one or both directions.

Trust and know that all is perfect and unfolding according to Divine Plan.

Her words are most reassuring.

I pause and take three more deep long breaths.

Modesty patiently waits for me to open my eyes.

She gives me a long loving embrace as she drifts into the ethers, leaving her presence deep within me.

I AM MODESTY

Memoir: I Am Modesty

One thing for sure, no one could ever accuse my sweet mother of being a *prude!* In fact, what most relatives and friends knew about her *for sure* is that she was beautiful, vivacious, open hearted, fun loving, totally compassionate and known to occasionally tell off-color jokes. As her child, I had the privilege of witnessing first hand that she was "virtually modest." And I mean to a fault.

Having grown up in unusually close quarters with a family of six, never did I see our mother in even her slip, which most women wore under their dresses in those early 20th-century days. That fact would probably seem quite unusual by today's standards, especially with the "let it all hang-out" acceptance as the norm in our society.

Mother was "well endowed" but no one would have ever suspected. She never flaunted or even eluded to any part of her body as though she was better than or privileged to have been given such a beautiful body. Her attitude toward her body was that it was a gift from God to be treasured and cherished and not to be overtly exposed.

That's how I grew up; with an appreciation for the virtue of modesty, which was reinforced in my parochial school training as well. So, you can imagine my shock when I began meeting friends from school and our neighborhood that had a whole different standard, or no standard at all in this realm.

The conversations and preoccupation of some of my friends with the size of another's breasts or the girth of their buttocks always left me feeling out in left field and totally speechless. Frankly, I could care less what anyone else's body dimensions measured. I remember thinking, "Who cares?" In our family, this was just not a topic for conversation. It was just a non-issue.

Not having been "well endowed" myself, it suddenly became an issue in high school. It seemed everyone was focused on who had the biggest breasts and the "best" rear-ends. For me it became a time of feeling very self-conscious and lesser than.

At a time when I was finally becoming less of an introvert socially, only to want to climb back into my invisible shell, I was facing all the body scrutiny. I now believe this is why so many young teenagers go through depression and loss of identity at this stage of their development. Evidently, this is a rite of passage that too many young people endure in order to come to self-acceptance.

At the age of fifteen years, it was the scrutiny I observed by fellow classmates and constant harassing toward those not considered "prime examples of what the norm should be" that became factors in my early exit from high school.

As I look back, the total lack of modesty on the part of some students was truly more than I could handle. Their focus on outward appearance, which also led to how well you dressed, was beyond foreign to me. I had always attended Catholic school where we wore uniforms.

Cashmere sweaters and white buck shoes were the status symbol of the era. To this day, I have never owned a cashmere sweater and have no desire to acquire one. I can still feel the sting of what they represented for me as well as for those who lacked these status adornments.

After quitting schooling in my sophomore year, when the toxic atmosphere of sexuality and importance of dress became more than my fragile psyche could handle, I went to work. This was the age before computers or convenient ways to check a person's correct age. Perhaps employers just didn't take the initiative or time to check credibility and I had always looked older than my age. It was easy for me to state that I was already sixteen years of age, which was a requirement.

To my delight, on entering the workforce as a clerk in a bank office, I found there was not the constant barrage of body comparisons which preoccupied students' minds. For me, that is still a very large issue. Maybe I am a prude. Women who find it necessary to expose their breasts as much as possible leave me dumbfounded. It's something I may never understand. I just know that as a young teen, this was always very confusing. Today's norms for exposing your body leaves me unimpressed and just a little puzzled.

As a CMT, Certified Massage Therapist, I have clients who have had breast implants say to me, "Do you want to see my breasts?" I try not to seem totally shocked, but I mean NO!

In massage training we were specifically schooled in how to drape so that our client is perfectly comfortable and never unnecessarily exposed. This is how I taught my students. Further-more, I respect my clients enough that I do not want to see those areas of their body that I consider not only private but sacred. Keep them for the special person with whom you will procreate or that special lover.

So, there you are! Today, modesty may not be a coveted

virtue, but the fact is that my mother taught me to be modest. This is the mode with which I am most comfortable. I AM MODEST! If that makes me a prude, so be it!

Mom's good friend Etha on the left, Momma on the right
In front of Dad's 1937 Oldsmobile
Dad bought this car with the money Mom saved when he was in the service.
Mom wanted to buy a house.

Chapter 11

Guided Meditation: Fearless

To prepare yourself for this meditation please read through its entirety. Then sit quietly and pay close attention to your breath. Begin to read again slowly following the guidance.

Closing my eyes, I pause and take three long, slow, deep breaths while feeling the life giving oxygen flow from my lungs out to my extremities and into all my vital organs.

In my mind's eye, I envision myself standing tall with my shoulders back and my eyes looking straight ahead at a future full of
my friend Courage
and excited anticipation.
My inner voice calls FEAR forward and there is an immediate response.
We draw close, standing toe to toe and gazing into one another's eyes.
With a deep sense of silence
I take three more, long, slow, deep breaths.

113

I am the first to speak as I look deeply
into FEAR'S eyes.

"Fear, I know you were in my life for a divine purpose since we
were introduced while I was still in the womb of my dearest
mother. There is no doubt you have served me like an overly
vigilant older sister who was entrusted with my safety.

Job well done!

Now, I allow you to unlock the chains that have bound us, and
you are finally free of this mission, which you approached with
deep dedication."

As Fear unlocks the chains, the recognizable figure of
TRUST,
wearing the garment of healthy caution approaches and with that
loving grin on his face, embraces me.

TRUST and I
stand shoulder to shoulder while holding hands.

We watch as Fear turns and walks away.

With one more final deep breath,

I open my eyes and declare

I AM FEARLESS

Memoir: I Am Fearless

Fearless! That is what I always wanted to be. Not to the extent that little three-year-old Dennis Chitwood was, but you know, living without the presence of fear in my day to day existence. Dennis was our neighbor's youngest child, while I was a preteen.

With his tow head, clear blue eyes and chubby little body, he would flex his muscles to impress and don his Superman cape before running around in circles, pretending to fly. Without a doubt, there was nothing cuter than his antics, which pulled at everyone's heart strings as we watched. We were amused and totally enthralled. That little boy would have inspired anyone observing to want to be fearless.

Hermetta, Dennis' mother, was in fact one of my childhood heroes. She had three older children and it was she who had most impressed me with the value of forgiveness. Aside from that, she was the embodiment of "motherhood." Hermetta was the omni-present mother at all of her children's school events, as well as supervising the neighborhood children's activities.

Regarding Dennis, you could hear his mom's exuberant laughter and giggles as she shared how "My littlest one leads his brother, Ronnie, and sisters, Judy and Annie into their dark room at night. He puts out protective arms, flexing his muscles and assures them he will keep them safe from harm." Doting mom that she was, Hermetta had shared, "At times I am concerned Dennis will leap off the second story porch, totally convinced that he can fly, just like Superman."

Nope, that's not the kind of fearless I had hoped to embody. Maybe it's more like the Victor Frankel kind of fearless. Remembering how he shared in his book, "A Man's Search for Meaning", he was able to stay in a place of trust with a knowing that the outcome was in a greater power's hands.

Perhaps this was the fearless (less fear) that I began to embody when early in our marriage, 1957, I convinced Bill into taking a risk and we purchased a piece of land in the hopes we would some-day be able to build a home.

I mean it was almost ludicrous; we could barely make our rent payments with both of us working. We already had our first child, Ted. Those were financially challenging times. We signed our names on the dotted line for the acreage and made monthly payments of fifty dollars for two years.

Then out of the blue, a friend, Liz Berry, led us to a non-profit organization where we signed another contract to have our home built for a very low mortgage interest. This little home was our paradise. We loved it and I knew it was divinely sent. All the painting inside and out became our pet project and allowed us to save money. The entire cost of having our home built was just fifteen thousand dollars, which seemed monumental at the time.

Yes, it was really scary. A real risk since we were now expecting our second child, Stephanie. I worked up until the very last moment in order to make ends meet. This for me was the kind of scary that made my heart race and tugged at my breath. We juggled bills, cut our food and utilities budget and prayed our way into home ownership. With fear and trepidation, we did it!

Shortly before we moved in, our first baby girl, Stephanie, was born. How well I remember, before moving in, painting for a

116

few hours then rushing to our apartment to shower before nursing our Missy (Stephanie). After having lived in rentals all my life, here we were with three bedrooms, one and a half baths, a beautiful kitchen and full basement.

The fact that we had to eat a lot of spam and peanut butter and jelly sandwiches out of necessity, in order to make our house payment, $87.50 mo., seemed a small sacrifice to fulfill our dream.

After about a year, my Sis and her wonderful husband, Dan and their three children moved in with us. The idea was they could help us financially while saving7 money to purchase the lot next door to ours where they eventually built their first home. We got along famously and rejoiced as they finally drew up the plans for their home. We all felt truly blessed. Bill and Dan both worked for the St. Louis County Police Dept. and Sis and I worked opposite shifts at the local Drug Store. Someone was always home to watch over our brood of five children between us. The entire set-up was more than ideal.

But dreams have a way of transitioning and giving way to nightmares. We lived happily in our home for a full five years while increasing our little family to five as we welcomed our precious second baby girl, Sylvia. While our other two children were planned and prayed for, she was our surprise.

In 1965, our first real crisis hit us smack between our eyes and we found it was time for us to move on if we were to survive our "Divine Tragedy (as shared in Chapter 19)."

Neither Bill nor I had been well traveled. Bill had seen a few other states as an active member of the National Guard. However, I had not ventured any farther than the neighboring state of Illinois for maybe a few hours. For us to make the humongous move from the Midwestern State of Missouri to the far Western State of California was no small jaunt in my book. Up to this time, this was the greatest risk of all. Even though my Mom and brothers would be there to welcome us, I can recall a huge chunk of terror being stuck in my throat.

At this point in my life, living with fear as my normal state seemed like the only way I knew how to function. Bill and I were making all these big grown-up decisions when inside I still felt like a scared-stiff child.

We sold our home and because the real estate market was down, we lost quite a bit of money on the deal. Just putting one foot in front of the other, we went for it. Many years prior, I had made the decision that the fear that had come with me to the planet would not block the destiny that I knew was just beyond my grasp.

We arrived in California in September 1965 and Mom and my brothers, Steve and Rich, and their families gave us all the support needed to get settled and start our new lives. Repeatedly, I found that taking risks was the only way to really build my sense of trust in my decisions.

Of course, sometimes I made disastrous decisions and my darling Bill became the victim of my folly, as did I. Like the time I talked him into investing in a piece of playground equipment (Tire-Play-A-Saurous). That really became a flop. We used our money to help finance someone else's dream and they made all the decisions. Not a good idea!

Though we landed in the West with just a meager savings, our goal was to be able to purchase a home as soon as possible. We both got jobs, working opposite hours so that one of us was

118

always home with our children. And of course, Mom was always there to help when needed.

Can you believe my darling, Bill, worked three part-time jobs until he could finally land a permanent job at the Naval Base in Concord, from which he retired thirty years later? The pioneers had nothing on the determination Bill displayed making sure our needs were provided. Within two years, we saved enough for a down payment on our second home purchase and after more than fifty years, we still reside at this "homestead."

To take a giant skip to the spring of 1973, at age thirty-six years, it found me going back to get my GED and then attending DVC, the Junior College. Not having graduated from high school had always been a "thorn in my side." This monumental step in my journey triggered the hugest transition and transformation my naive spiritual life could have imagined.

I mean, by making this move, it meant we were now paired down to one income, which was insane. It is difficult to explain. I can only say there was a knowing and a calling that this was the time I was supposed to follow my inner guidance. You may call it intuition. It was time for me to get onto the path I was to follow even if it meant another financial hardship.

Bill and I began tithing, which is a biblical term for allotting ten percent of your income for charity. Our already overextended budget shrunk when I quit work. Now we began digging deep into that faithful promise when you give from your first fruits you are more than ten times blessed. It was not our intention to put our faith to the test, but…Without going into a very long dissertation, I can tell you that a financial miracle happened in very short order. Bill received a totally unexpected windfall from

119

his work, due to a class-action lawsuit that awarded all the employees several thousand dollars.

You may say, as some skeptics have, "Well of course that would have happened anyway." You may be right! However, I believe it is all about timing. My belief is that miracles happen when you are aligned and recognize a power greater than your self is working on your behalf.

This unexpected blessing allowed us to pay off some bills that made it possible for me to pursue my objective without the undue stress of guilt for having quit my job. At this stage of my life, I began to recognize that a higher power was cooperating with my life decisions, or maybe it was the other way around. All I know for sure is I was now living with much less fear.

Our children's welfare and Bill's and my life decisions were now more and more entrusted to "The Source" or Creator...whatever you understand that to be. For me, it was the Angels, Jesus, and all the Saints, a Heavenly Father, on and on. It was all the divine connections I had been taught by the Sisters, which I had at one time discarded when I allowed myself to throw my faith out the window because it wasn't working the way I thought it should.

Oh, I had always continued to attend church, and for a time it was to be on my terms. I was going to be in control, but when I had my breakdown, I had all the evidence of how that disastrous plan worked out.

Armed with my recovered and transformed faith and trust, I ventured into the realm of striving to complete my academic education, which my whole being longed for.

I had made a commitment to my spiritual progress and

thought that was all that was needed. The Divine Spirit had a much deeper and broader plan. It was at this time that I went through a huge spiritual transformation, which landed me in the psychiatric ward of Kaiser Hospital in Martinez, California.

During this time, I began taking inventory of the person I had become, living without forgiveness in my heart, and my whole world collapsed. I found I was asking myself, "Who am I really"? At the time, it seemed like the worst possible experience was happening to me as I met "My dark night of the soul" The title of the book by the Catholic Saint, John of the Cross.

It seemed to fit my deep dark depression to a tee. Looking back, I know this time was the greatest gift that saved my soul. Without it, I believe my life decisions would have led me down a path of destruction. Sounds dramatic, but I discovered that's what life is, one big drama.

A full year was spent recovering and realigning my body and mind to fit into the spiritual being I was becoming. Still not knowing what that meant, it didn't matter. Trust became my most treasured virtue.

My first thirty-six years had been spent on this planet without the virtue of trust. Today, that thought makes me shudder. It is now incomprehensible that I chose fear over trust. It is my suspicion, at milestones in my life, I was offered other ways of responding and my pride and lack of trust prompted me to reject them.

Looking back at that early memory when little Dennis Chitwood was demonstrating his bravery antics, mimicking his hero, Superman, I realize in his innocence he was teaching all of us watching the virtue of TRUST! I labeled it FEARLESS! It

121

took me many years to grasp his lesson. Once I learned to trust, I discovered I was not only living with less fear, but I too had become FEARLESS!

Hermetta Chitwood
Dennis' Mommy
One of the most inspiring and forgiving persons
that I had the privilege of knowing.

Chapter 12

Guided Meditation: Discernment

To prepare yourself for this meditation please read through its entirety. Then sit quietly and pay close attention to your breath. Begin to read again slowly following the guidance.

I close my eyes and focus on my breathing
With three long deep breaths,
I allow myself to be transported into the center of my heart.
You my friend Discernment show up at the most unexpected times.

Often, I hardly recognize you. After all these years, you would think making decisions with you and the help of our friend Wisdom would become easier.

I take three more long deep breaths, exhaling each breath slowly.

Yes, it is true I can sometimes see you so clearly that the right decision is made spontaneously and I feel sooo good about it.

But you know, some of the
"best for all concerned" decisions
seem to be cloaked in a darkened room where the light switch is

123

either missing or so well hidden that I grope blindly,
searching until exhaustion almost defeats me.

I try to weigh the possibilities and what I finally realize is:

I am still stuck in the mode of fearing to make a mistake.

Then, I remember what our friend

Wisdom
has instructed me;

"There really are no mistakes, only opportunities to learn."

I take three more long deep breaths, exhaling each breath slowly.

With this profound teaching tucked assuredly in my heart,

I can now go forward knowing that there will always be forks in
the road.

But all roads have destinations that will broaden my scope of life
experiences.

They will all allow me to fulfill my destiny and complete my life
journey as designed.

My higher self reminds me;

"Seek first the kingdom and all else will be added to you."
Matthew 6:33

With a deep breath, I open my eyes.

Thank you, my friend Discernment, you and Wisdom never fail
me.

Memoir: I Am Discernment

I mean, who knew there was another whole dimension to "Judgment"? This is what I grew up with: "Judge not that you not be judged." Matthew 7:1-3 It was that statement which set up a kind of constant bickering within my head between Discernment (even though I didn't recognize this term) and Judgment. Who the heck did these two think they were setting up residence as though they had paid the mortgage on my brain?

Those two voices, Discernment and Judgment, were like young siblings vying for my attention. Not sure of their gender, but I'm absolutely sure they both had some kind of a hyper attention disorder. Neither was content unless my mental wheels were spinning. Apparently, this was the birthing of the conscience that the nuns told me I had to examine regularly.

Then too, there was Mom's inner recording reminding me of the wise teachings of the church, "If you can't say something nice, don't say anything at all." Ephesians 4:29 OMG, now that I look back, impressionable child that I was, taking everything I heard literally and as the "Gospel truth", trying to censor my thoughts kept me on extreme vigilant alert.

Whenever I was making a snap decision about someone or something that didn't fit into my frame of reference, those two inner siblings took the liberty to challenge one another. Visualize a boxing ring and you get the picture.

Believing the nun's insistence that every "good Catholic" examines their conscience before going off to sleep every night made me a prime target for anxiety. I was fearful that I may have

125

forgotten to ask forgiveness for some offense I had committed. After all, wasn't I told that I was supposed to love everybody and I was acutely aware that for me this was just not the case.

From the very beginning, even as a child, I recognized there were certain people whose actions disturbed me to no end. It was these beings that I would strive to eliminate from my day-to-day interactions. In fact, my preference was *to avoid them altogether.* The most blaring example would be my grandmother, Liz, who always seemed to be present.

Being my mom's mother, she wanted to be as close to Mom as possible. In my later life I became aware that Grandma was trying to make up for the neglect and abuse she had visited on my Mom as a child. She was often our care provider while Mom worked. It was no secret that this woman did not like my sister nor me. Almost all of Grandma's interactions with Sis and I proved to be negative and harsh. Based on what I had been taught, my thoughts about her would be considered "judgments." The truth was I just flat out "did not like her." This awareness set up within me, huge feelings of guilt and unrest.

It wasn't until as an adult I began to recognize that Grandma was still a very injured child who had never matured and her tongue lashings toward my sister and me were the result of her own deep wounds.

Compassion, Understanding and the nourishment of Wisdom finally allowed me to become aware that these early childhood conclusions in Grandma's regard, were in fact the birthing of Discernment.

Tempering my judgments toward her and others I have judged, with Compassion, has allowed me to create a zone of peace.

126

Knowing that yes, there are people with whom my personality and theirs will probably never mesh, gives me and them permission to be our true selves. Even Jesus made the statement "Father, I do not pray for the whole world, but for those you have given me." John 17:9

I love my dear friend Discernment. She has lifted a huge weight from my shoulders. Love everybody, not, *like* everybody, is the admonition. Discernment has taught me the difference. Even in my own family, while I believe we each have something to teach one another by our challenges, some of us have totally different inclinations toward life.

We may vote differently, practice different faiths, like different music and TV programs, on an on...but we can still love one another. We may not choose to spend the holidays together because of our differences, but Discernment keeps us from feeling offended and setting up expectations that make each other uncomfortable. Children could grasp these deep principles when they are raised with them and what a blessedly different world would result. Thank you, thank you, Discernment. You make my life so much more enjoyable.

To cite another example from the other end of the spectrum: A vivid memory of having been totally crushed on discovering two people with whom I closely interacted absolutely disliked me. I was devastated.

(LOL)!! At this stage of my life, it is fodder for having a big belly laugh. However, back then, it was incomprehensible. Can you imagine the gigantic ego that would surmise that everyone would just love me and want to associate with me?

That was such a huge lesson. Surmising that I was pretty

much able to fit in with most any situation or diverse group, here it was hitting me smack in the face; the unthinkable. There are people who dislike me with a passion. OMG, how can I go on? (Giggle)! I was so flabbergasted that I made specific appointments with each of these two to inquire exactly what it was about me that caused them to dislike me so vehemently.

Both were very candid and explicit in their responses and for the most part they revealed that I reminded them of someone in their past history that they found most offensive. "You are just too over the top in expressing your faith." I must remind you; this was a time when the new dimensions of spirituality had been revealed or discovered by me.

Being beyond excited and bubbling over with effervescence with my new found faith proved more than many could tolerate. Closing my eyes, I can still visualize my exploding upon each scene as though I had just found the pot of gold at the end of the rainbow. Even I now know it was a "bit much."

The Charismatic movement was finding its way into the Catholic communities. For me, it was a most freeing time. In my mind, the windows and doors of the church had just been opened wide and the presence of the Holy Spirit seemed so tangible, it felt like I could touch the joy that rushed in.

Every sense of my body was tingling as though I could see, smell, taste and feel the abundance of love that was brought in with this new awareness. Assuming everyone else felt this same "rush" ...Not so! While there wasn't an "I found it!" bumper sticker on my car, when I saw those stickers on other cars, I wanted to roll down my car window and wave and shout, "Me too"!

Get the picture? Obnoxiously, deliriously beyond joyful was my "modus-operandi." Once it was discovered that some people hated my new- found exuberance, like some of my family and these two people who belonged to my Bible Study Group and our Marriage Encounter Group, it was as if someone let all the helium out of my self-inflated Mylar balloon.

Remember the movie, PATCH ADAMS, where Robin Williams plays a doctor and is disliked by another doctor because he was "just too happy"? Man, I could really relate to that. I got it loud and clear. Sometimes that happy vibration is just a bit more than can be tolerated on a daily basis.

Perhaps those who wanted to avoid me like the plague either correctly judged me wacky or *discerned* I was a little off kilter. Whichever it was, both would be close to correct. For a time, I was definitely not the person I had been. It took me well over a year after my epiphany to come back to earth and find grounding.

That year was spent meditating, exercising, reading self-help books and studying scripture while striving to find my ideal equilibrium. Once I could *discern* how to fit back into the normal stream of everyday life and not be an offensive "bible thumper", I began to recognize the pendulum had swung way too far from left to right. The world had already been "saved", from the Churches perspective. It really wasn't my mission. All I had to do was love and appreciate all the dwellers.

For sure, I have great tolerance for people that others often shun, because of this over-zealous, self- righteous attitude. *Been there done that*, is my motto when I see people that display these behaviors.

As an example, a dear young man who is a close friend, father and wonderful husband, has suddenly become a mirror image of the classic "born again" Christian. Wouldn't I just love to be able to help him to find that equilibrium that is so necessary for others to hear him? There is an internal knowing that the energy must run its course and somewhere along the line he will settle down and realize he too is not called to "save the world."

It is Discernment that comes to the rescue and finally introduces Wisdom to us individuals who, at some point, assume we have all the answers. Somehow, we have to make fools of ourselves or fall flat on our faces before we wake up and calm down.

Sadly, another friend of mine finally left her husband when his overly zealous nature became beyond tolerable. I am most grateful that my husband, Bill, with his patience rode out the storm.

Patience is one of the necessary virtues needed to recognize this as a path some of us have to travel. For most, it isn't a permanent mode. It's just a time of transition and transformation until we can embrace the gift of

Discernment.

Chapter 13

Guided Meditation: Deepened Faith

To prepare yourself for this meditation please read through its entirety. Then sit quietly and pay close attention to your breath. Begin to read again slowly following the guidance.

Closing my eyes and taking three long deep breaths
I instruct my body to begin to relax from the top of my head to the tips of my toes.
I pause and wait for that sweet relaxed feeling.
My dear Deepened Faith, you are always less than a half a breath away.
You are felt deep in the crevices of all my muscles and bones.
Like a river, you flow through my body, bringing light and life to every cell.
I pause and take three more long deep breaths.
You remind me that the angels are whispering in my ear throughout the day. Their mission is to enhance the signs around me; calling my attention to be mindful of their presence.
You, my dear Deepened Faith, are my lifeline to Hope, which

131

allows me to expect miracles along my path.

As I journey through my day, you nudge me to acknowledge that

I AM

a child of the Most High God/Goddess.

Without you, Deepened Faith,

my life would have no meaning or purpose.

Thank you for being one of my dearest friends.

I love you,

Deepened Faith.

Opening my eyes, I begin to look for miracles.

Memoir: I AM Deepened Faith

Fear gripped me as I climbed over bodies, pushed open the heavy limo door, leapt out, terrified out of my mind by the crash that landed us in the dark recesses of the warehouse district of downtown St. Louis. Running for my life, not knowing where, suddenly the stark realization hit me: I was in a shadowy, dank alleyway between tall brick buildings in the dead of night.

The musty smelling cobblestones beneath my feet were wet and slippery causing me to lose my balance and almost fall repeatedly. My heart was in my throat and I couldn't swallow. The terror of thinking: *My Dad is going to kill me if he finds out I got into a car with strangers*, consumed me. His foreboding wrath was way more terrifying than the predicament in which I found myself.

My prayer was short and swift, "Angels, save me"! Still running, as I approached the end of the alley, there was a dark figure in a long dark coat. His shadowed face spoke to me, "Get into that cab and don't ever get picked up again!"

To this day, I have to ask myself what the odds were that a cab would be at the end of the deserted alleyway and someone forcefully directing me to "get into" it and prepaying the fare. This all took place in seconds.

I would like to think this was an apparition; a heavenly sent angel or some kind of alien. Closer to the truth is that it was probably one of the young men who was also an occupant in the limo who saw me jump out and run down the alleyway. Apparently, he circled around the building, anticipating where I would end up. I mean, that is just my guess.

The whole event happened so quickly, with my responding only from an adrenal rush, propelled by an overabundance of fear. It really doesn't matter, either-way, that young man will always be remembered as the "Guardian Angel" who solidified my deepened faith.

The cab driver never spoke to me on the way home and delivered me safely at least thirty or forty miles away from where the accident occurred. My prayers of gratitude stormed heaven for the entire fifty or so minute ride. Upon arrival, I jumped out quickly, not even sure if I thanked this man. Shock was still overtaking me.

Grateful that my household was quiet, with everyone already asleep. With my thoughts still racing, I crept into the safety of my bed. There was to be no peaceful rest that night as I began to reconstruct the scenario leading up to this horrendous occurrence.

Peggy, my closest friend, invited me to join her and Pat, her sister, and three other friends on an adventure to Forest Park Highlands Roller Rink. I say "adventure" because there was a neighborhood rink, Downs Roller Rink, much closer. For some reason, on this Friday evening, these young ladies wanted to experience something more challenging.

Peggy and I were the youngest of the crowd by at least two or three years. Joan, who was around seventeen years, was the oldest. She was considered from my point of view very "worldly" since she smoked and used four letter words rather fluently. There was a sense that Joan wasn't too thrilled that Peggy and I were tagging along but tolerated us because Pat was her best friend.

At fourteen years, Peggy was a year older than me. Both she and I had always looked older for our age, but we were still pretty green when it came to street smarts. Pat and Peggy's mom would probably never have approved, nor would my Mom, had they known we were going all the way into St. Louis, thirty-five miles away, with Joan.

So here we were, all taking a risk we knew was not OK but feeling excited that we were getting away with something. In addition, I had borrowed my sister's shoe roller skates without her permission. Obviously, this was an accident waiting to happen.

Our destination, over an hour, was a couple of buses and a streetcar away. It all seemed worth the effort once we put on our skates and waltzed off on the beautiful gleaming floors. Luxury like this was more than we were accustomed, and the music sets were more challenging and fun.

We met so many new people which made the whole experience a huge success. Joan with her gorgeous blond hair and Pat with her knock-out figure, drew young men like flies. In turn, they lavished attention on us younger ladies as well. Peggy and I were feeling very grown-up. All in all, we gauged this evening a memorable event and couldn't wait to rehash it on the ride home.

The first leg of our journey home was uneventful on a public service bus, which delivered us to the first stop. While waiting for a street car, a long black limousine pulled up and offered to give us a ride. Our first response was "no way." But then Joan engaged with them in conversation and soon informed us that she knew one of the young men through her brother and the ride would be safe.

Half believing her, we all piled in and excitedly continued to converse and laugh. Before we knew it, the driver began driving erratically and we became aware that someone in another car had challenged him to race.

My paranoia kicked in immediately. Driving with my Dad while he was inebriated over many years had instilled within me a fear of fast driving that lingers deep inside me to this day. Swerving around corners, screeching tires and then just as suddenly as it all began there was a terrible thud that stopped us in our tracks when we plowed into some immovable unseen object.

Screaming, confusion and my account as relayed at the beginning of this writing followed. When I leapt out of the vehicle, my purse and Sis' beautiful shoe skates were left behind. All I cared about taking at that moment was my life.

Laying there in my bed in the dark of night, I felt like I had just passed through a time zone. How a joyful, fun-filled evening had in the twinkling of an eye plunged to the depths of this terrifying horror story made my head spin. Wrapped in the comfort of prayer through the night, the anticipation of another heavy shoe falling in the morning kept me from the much-desired slumber.

But it didn't fall! When I got in touch with Peggy at school a couple of days later (we had only a four-party telephone line at the time, no way would I have discussed any part of this event on that device.) we didn't even discuss the accident. To this day, I have no idea how the others got home or what transpired after my abrupt exit.

Fortunately, no one was injured. We had been packed in so

tightly, I guess we all cushioned one another. All I know for sure is that this was another big chunk of the deepened faith that was to become the foundation for my life philosophy.

My first initiation into a deepened faith way of navigating my life came much earlier in my childhood while at a school picnic. In recalling the sounds and tempo of the Chain of Rocks Amusement Park, it still has the power to transport me to the many times we celebrated that annual school event.

On this memorable day, our Mom was not able to accompany Sis, Rich and me. Consequently, Grandma Liz chaperoned us as we began our journey on the long-dreaded, one-and-a half-hour streetcar ride. The swaying of the car always precipitated within me a nauseous response. My first hour at the picnic was usually spent with me crying and wanting to throw up. (This did not make Grandma happy). You got it; I was a pain in the a_ _.

My sister and brother went off with their friends, leaving Grandma and me to explore the park together. At one point, she took my hand and led me to a long line. Watching as the huge Ferris wheel turned, I could hear the shouts and screams of the passengers enjoying their excursion.

Eventually, we reached the head of the line and I began to realize that Grandma was taking me on this fearful ride. Pulling back, I protested. Grandma grabbed me, ushered me to a swinging seat and plopped me down firmly. The man quickly locked the bar and we were on our way to the next slot as he swiftly secured another rider.

It is important to clarify right now there was not a single sign of a brave bone in my skinny little, five-year-old, waif-looking body. In fact, I was pathetically fearful of everything. Grandma's intense dislike of me was, I am sure, tied to this fact and she made no pretense of hiding it.

As we began our ascent up the wheel, I again protested and was quickly silenced with Grandma's hand over my mouth, breathing into my ear "shut up." By the time we got to the top of the Ferris wheel, Grandma decided to rock the seat, which prompted me to let out the most horrifying sobs and cried out, "GOD SAVE ME!" I can still see Grandma's enraged red face and angry piercing eyes devouring me. Whenever I see a picture of a charging bull, it reminds me of Grandma's intent in that moment.

By the time we completed just one rotation, the Ferris wheel was stopped, and the man opened the bar. He heard my crying sobs and intervened. Grandma's attempt to restrain me was futile. Running as fast as my legs would carry me among the hundreds of people, I found my Sis in the penny arcade.

After telling her my story, she allowed me to cling to her for the rest of the day. Together, we dodged Grandma until it was time to head home. My Sis was always my hero.

I am quite sure Grandma didn't bother to look for me. She was probably relieved I was no longer her responsibility. Even on the long ride home, Grandma didn't sit near us. While my Sis was my savior on many occasions when Grandma was dishing out her mistreatment, my deep faith began to grow by leaps and bounds as I frequently called on the angels, saints and Jesus prior to being rescued.

A recent news article reported a man shared that he believes he was spared in a plane crash when he cried out, "Jesus

Save Me"! There were others who perished in that crash. His belief reinforced my faith as I read it. Testing my faith is not something I practice, but you can be sure that supplication, "Jesus Save Me"! is ready and on the tip of my tongue at a moment's notice.

I AM SO GRATEFUL FOR
DEEPENED FAITH

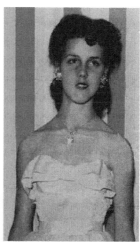

Peggy Ryan, Best Friend
before & during High School

Grandma Liz and Me~ 1939
She may have actually liked me then

Me & Sis ~ 1957
Sis was always my protector & hero

Chapter 14

Guided Meditation: Honesty

To prepare yourself for this meditation please read through its entirety. Then sit quietly and pay close attention to your breath. Begin to read again slowly following the guidance.

Sitting quietly with my eyes closed

I take three long deep breaths, consciously exhaling, slowly and deliberately.

My Sacred Heart knows this truth:

I am pure

Honesty.

This is my divine birthright.

However, as I stand at the threshold of my heart, the reality of this truth needs to be conveyed to all the cells of my body.

I will send ripples of this truth by way of my nervous system, like a herald of glad tidings.

I pause and take three long deep breaths visualizing this message flowing like an electrical current telecasting the truth that I AM pure Honesty

142

It matters not that the voice of my inner accuser reminds me of the times I have not lived in my integrity and expressed my truth.

Taking three more slow breaths,

I go deeper into my heart with the message:

Today is a brand new day, the first day of the rest of my life and I choose from this day forward to allow the

Angel of Honesty

to help me live my birthright of Honesty.

My prayer today is:

Dearest Angel of Honesty, I believe you are with me empowering me to live from my truth.

Remind me to stay in my heart and to picture the ripples of Honesty flowing into my cells.

I take three more slow deep breaths and open my eyes.

My inner voice says with conviction,

I AM HONESTY

I will be Honest in all my dealings

One day at a time.

Memoir: I AM Honesty

"He's a straight shooter" or "She shoots straight from the hip." For sure you have heard these expressions. They could have been conveying a story about my Mom, who had the uncanny ability to look you directly in the eyes and detect the least amount of untruth and calling you on it.

You would have thought she was a Sagittarius in the Zodiac system because that is a trait these December people are said to possess. They are said to be painfully honest. The main difference would have to be that Mom was also very sensitive and diplomatic. She could coax the truth from someone while conveying that she was on their side.

Mom was a Libra in that same system, having the symbol of balanced scales, which indicate "fairness." Yep, that would describe Mom. She epitomized fairness in all her dealings. How she ever got paired with my Dad, who seemed hell bent on pioneering a trail for his life journey by taking every shortcut and dodging bullets of truth, while building outposts where he only narrowly and miraculously survived.

Perhaps that is one of the reasons why Dad was so conspicuously absent in our home. Mom's crystal-clear clarity, "calling a spade a spade", may have been more than my Dad could bear. It was like trying to cram darkness into the corner of a brilliantly lighted space. Home was definitely Mom's domain. Dad's domain was the corner tavern with his "cronies" as Mom called them.

144

Difficult to comprehend my parents' marriage surviving over twenty-nine years. Mom was committed to this "sacred union." Excuse me, from the perspective of the children produced in this time period, this coupling was anything but sacred. Mom's philosophy was, "half a father was better than no father at all."

Tremendous influence was impressed on the family by the church at this time. Divorce was not even considered an option and opportunities for women to earn an income were very limited.

Honest woman to the core, this had to be a tortuous facade for Mom to present to Dad's family. Her deep respect for Grandma, Dad's mother, I believe caused Mom to hold her tongue until and as she stated, "I vowed to bide my time until all you children were married."

A fact that was not disclosed to me until I, as the youngest child, was planning my wedding and departure. Mom confided to me that shortly after my wedding, she would be filing for the long overdue divorce she had been planning for many years.

Looking into my Mother's clear-blue eyes, I knew only too well how often they got her into insufferable trouble from an insanely jealous, insecure spouse. The sacrifices Mom endured for the love of her children were many.

When Mom spoke to anyone, she looked directly into their eyes. This drove my Dad crazy. Most of their tirade arguments were over some suspected flirtatious conversation Mom had that evening with either a male relative or a friend. Truth be known, if Dad had taken the time to look directly into Mom's clear-blue eyes, he could have seen her honest innocence. His own eyes were too often clouded by the effects of alcohol.

Mom had a personality and manner that drew everyone to her. Conversing came as easily to her as breathing. Telling jokes and laughing were her trademark. Everyone else saw her sincerity, genuineness and forthright honesty.

I suspect that Dad, being five years her senior, wasn't aware of what a jewel he had mined at her fragile age of fourteen years. By the time he became cognitive of her rare beauty and traits, he must have recognized he was way in over his head.

Without the skills or maturity to allow Mom to take the lead, he was threatened and intimidated beyond his coping level. He chose to hide in alcohol and used measures to demean and tear her down. Sadly, Dad sabotaged their marriage and destined it to failure from the very beginning.

In all their children's development, Mom was our strong fortress. She was the rudder in our storms, the safe port from near collisions and provided the map from which to navigate. She held us to a strict code of honesty and integrity and was our living role model. One look into her clear-blue eyes and we knew to recalculate if we were plotting too far off course.

The ache in my heart can still be felt when remembering the time, I was less than truthful in relaying a story to Mom. Her retort, "You speak with a forked tongue", elevated my consciousness. I can't even remember the exact incident I was sharing, but her rebuke is indelibly engraved in my psyche. It reminds me to speak cautiously when inclined to be critical of someone's behavior.

Wishing I had the kind of record for honesty that Mom had is an understatement. As I take inventory, I recognize that a deep-seated fear of who I was and consequences I had seen my siblings suffer, often propelled me to be less than honest.

Coming to terms with who I am, honesty has become one of the most freeing attributes or qualities I can claim from Mom's legacy. Accepting that I am more than basically an honest person, I strive to stay the steady course Mom, the Master Shipman, plotted. Because I am my Mother's daughter and by the grace of God, I can accept that at my core.

I AM HONESTY

When Momma looked at you with those Clear-Blue Eyes, you knew you had better be telling the truth.

MOMMS'S KIDS~ HER PRIDE AND JOY

Brother Steve's Family ~ 1966
Patsy, Steve, Laura & Steven

Sis's Family~ David, Sis, Dan, Cliff & Micki (1965)

Brother Rich's Family ~ 1966
Front: Debbie, Patsy, Denise, and Richie
Back: Rich and Pat

149

Bill's & My Family (Still Audrey) ~ 1969
Front: Sylvia, Audrey, Stephanie, Back: Bill and Ted

2004 ~ Rich, Steve, A Diamond, Sis
Steve's 75th Birthday Party, Baldwin Park in Concord, CA

Chapter 15

Guided Meditation: Fortitude

To prepare yourself for this meditation please read through its entirety. Then sit quietly and pay close attention to your breath. Begin to read again slowly following the guidance.

Sweet Fortitude, you who are by far more valuable than either talent or genius,

I welcome and invite you to coach me in your ways.

Pausing, I close my eyes, take three long, slow, deep breaths.

My Sacred Heart is informed to get ready to greet the Prince of all that is worth accomplishing.

Without Fortitude, all would be lost.

I pause and take another three-long slow, breaths.

My inner vision carries me into my Sacred Heart where a myriad of dedicated people are marching up a majestic mountain to honor the

Prince of Fortitude.

There at the summit sits the humblest of servants robed in white silk with a shining crown of gold and jewels. There is no pretension, only joy filling the prince's demeanor. He is waving, cheering and welcoming each and every person, including myself as we reach the summit.

It's hard to be sure who is more joy filled, the prince or those of us who have patiently and persistently accomplished our goals.

What a grand celebration this is!

With three long deep breaths I sit quietly and just savor this scene in my sacred heart for a few minutes.

Our prince reaches out and embraces each of us individually. He then touches each one's forehead and anoints us with the aroma of freshly cut heather sacred oil.

My soul has a knowing that staying the course is truly a worthy quest

As I slowly return to consciousness, there is an awareness that Fortitude is not only the mentor but also the role model and advocate.

He makes me proud to say over and over

I AM FORTITUDE

Memoir: I Am Fortitude

The Nuns drilled them into the gills of our receptive brains: Wisdom, Understanding, Counsel, Fortitude, Knowledge, Piety and Awe and Wonder in His Presence (the last formerly being Fear of The Lord); all the "Seven Gifts of the Holy Spirit." Like a sponge, I soaked them up, thirsting for the truth of my existence. We were told these gifts were freely given for the asking and who doesn't like free stuff?

Hook, line and sinker, every word was swallowed. Yes, the Nuns were truly fishers for the Church. Though heavy handed at times, using casting line that was perhaps a little too weighted for the young, guppy-like children in their charge. However, there is no regret in my having had a parochial foundation formed by these dedicated, stern fisher women.

Between my chaotic home life and the absence of my hard-working mother, the Catholic School environment provided a kind of protected aquarium type of condition in which to learn and grow. While it did not offer the tenderness of gentle nourishing love, it did convey the mental acknowledgment "there is a better place that you are being prepared to swim toward."

It came with the promise of a Heavenly Father who would love me unconditionally. Loving me so much, "He even knew the number of hairs on my head." Luke 12:7

Believing that kind of love awaited me, my young heart was so filled with hope that I was transformed from a fragile guppy into a strong, agile salmon. Swimming upstream, I was conditioned to become resilient with the capability to withstand

153

the rushing current of life to eventually spawn my own progeny.

Little did I realize the gift of Fortitude was being demonstrated in our home life by the very presence of my dearest Mother. "Fortitude: courage in facing pain, danger or trouble; firmness of spirit" … is the definition the dictionary provides.

Mother was like a strong fortress, shielding her children from the harshest realities of life. Without her tenacity and perseverance, the ability to stay in a state of grace fueled by the love she had for her children, only God/Goddess knows where we would have landed and what would have become of us.

Fortitude is so profoundly demonstrated and modeled to me by our son, Ted. He used the martial arts to overcome many obstacles on his life journey to become a "Black Belt" in Karate; owning a school and teaching others to use this method to find their highest purpose. Observing and listening, I, too, learn.

Ted's son, our grandson, Alexander, also has this gift of Fortitude as he persevered through various stages of "learning the hard way." Today he has become the greatest of dads to our great-grandson, James, and owns his little slice of heaven in Washington State. Alexander and his wife, J'Me, are turning their property into a horse ranch and farmland. Miracles are happening every day. Thank you, Fortitude.

Perhaps our children and grandchildren are our greatest teachers for this virtue: Our daughter, Stephanie, even after her debilitating stroke, persisted in achieving her associate degree. Our daughter Sylvia, in her mid-fifties, left the corporate world and accomplished her certificate in the Fashion Design Industry. Our grandson, Brandon, is nearing his completion of becoming a Computer Engineer after serving in Iraq. Ryan, our middle grandson, helps run a successful resort in the state of Washington while stepping forward and forging his chosen role as a "stay-at-home Dad"; giving our great-grandson, Jax, the very best of role-modeling. Our youngest grandson, Shane, completed training as a long-haul truck driver and gets to experience the challenges of the open road while photographing and cataloguing the awesome scenery.

Yes, Fortitude is demonstrated endlessly if we take the time to observe and appreciate the accomplishments of others.

Embracing this virtue of fortitude, in myself, did not come easy. The nuns had accomplished their mission to scale and fillet their young guppies, trimming every trace of vanity and pride down to the bone. To recognize any good quality or attribute in one's self was a source of "sinfulness that would make a black hole in your heart", said the nuns. Under their tutelage, it was most difficult to escape with any sense of self-esteem.

There were those who rebelled, which brings to mind my dearest sister, Sis. Her strong spirit could defy gravity and got her into many confrontations with the nuns. But that was not a role I was conditioned to play. As the silent observer biding my time listening, I became the witness who trusted the phrase, "this too shall pass", while navigating without receiving too many bruises from crashing into the pervading hard knocks on my way up the stream of life.

Cultivating Fortitude or perseverance was a by-product of my style of swimming through life. It was as natural as breathing, although unrecognized in myself until I was on the receptive end of many years of comments from peers, friends, teachers and relatives. "You are so patient, you have such perseverance, you are such a dedicated person", were statements directed toward me by friends and sometimes even family. Mostly the comments ran off me like water rushing over my outer scales unable to penetrate the armor that protected me from the nuns so called, "sin of pride."

Finally, maturity gave me permission to integrate this Gift of The Holy Spirit. Recognizing not to accept this gift of Fortitude was an insult to the spirit that dwells deep within me as it does in each human being. I can now say "with humility" (an oxymoron), I have the gift of Fortitude and will use it to better my life as well as the life of others.

This gift of Fortitude is evident in many areas of my life: over sixty-four years of marriage to my wonderful husband, Bill, completing my massage training and then creating a massage school, running a Holistic Health Center for over twenty-five years, living in the same home for over fifty years and the love, understanding and appreciation I feel toward my family friends, neighbors and clients. I believe all this is the direct consequence of acknowledging and accepting the Gift of Fortitude.

Then of course there was having stayed the course in helping to raise our grandsons after our daughter Stephanie's stroke. Looking back, I recall the messages from the doctor and nurses, who I realize now were just trying to protect both Bill and me.

However, their advice was unthinkable, not even able to register in our consciousness. "You'll have to make a choice: either put the children into foster care and take care of your daughter or put your daughter into a care facility until you see how far she will progress and take care of the children."

"WHAT? Did we just hear correctly?" There wasn't a

chance in HE_ _ that Bill and I would choose either of the options offered. They had even gone so far as to give us lists of facilities where we could begin to set into motion the process of acquiring care providers or foster care for our grandsons OMG! They would have to cut off both our arms before we would surrender our grandsons or our daughter if there was any chance at all that we could meet the challenge.

And we did! Stephanie was in the hospital for four months and when we brought her home, she needed vigilant care for at least another couple of years. It was the test of a lifetime, but we believed, and we managed.

"Tough Love" was sometimes the order of the day as we challenged our daughter to progress. She had to learn all the basics from eating, walking, and speaking to grooming herself and dressing.

At one point in her process a friend said to me, "If you don't make her get out of that wheelchair, she will never walk." With our hearts breaking, we moved her bedroom upstairs and forced her to crawl up the stairs to her room. She was beyond angry with us. It was an embarrassment for her to have her children see her doing this. Within weeks, Stephanie was using a walker and putting forth the effort to overcome the stairs in an upright position. She then began walking around our kitchen table to strengthen her legs. What a fearless warrior she became.

Fortitude became evident in Stephanie, too, as she faithfully went to physical therapy twice a week. It was a whole new universe of learning how to navigate in her now physically challenged world. All this required a constant vigilance over, not only her schedules and making sure she practiced her therapy at home, but also making sure our small grandsons, ages two years, four years and nine years, had their needs met.

Perhaps that is my biggest regret: not being able to provide all the special parental attention required to assure each child's individuality was recognized. Thank heavens for our youngest daughter, Sylvia, and niece, Judy, who filled in where the cracks were widest. Still, the boys being short- changed became evident as they reached their rebellious teens.

All I know for sure is that Bill and I gave it our very best shot. One of our greatest compliments came when our grandson's paternal grandmother, Nelda, Stephanie's mother-in-law, said, "Thank God for you and Bill, I could not have done it."

The love shown to Bill and me from our own parents and the strong faith force fed to me by the nuns paid off. Without that foundation of Fortitude, our precious grandsons may have been abandoned and not have known the strong family support in which they were raised.

Our sweet Stephanie is still totally paralyzed on her left side. She walks and speaks haltingly, but she was able to drive a car for many years when we had her car adapted. She works part-time for the local Junior College, Diablo Valley College. Her mind is as sharp as ever and she thoroughly enjoys her accounting position. Her supervisors love her since she is such a joy to be around.

Her doctor had told us, "This kind of operation will either leave Stephanie totally depressed or euphoric." In the beginning, her euphoria was a problem and she would laugh at the most inopportune times. Example: as the Host (Communion) was being raised during Sunday Mass she burst out laughing, etc., etc.

You get the picture (not good). Eventually, she became able to control her laughter response. We just thank heaven she is always happy, smiling and does still spread her infectious laughter.

At this writing, Stephanie's children, our grandsons, are now ages thirty-seven, thirty-one and twenty-nine. As I look back at the task accomplished, even I am astonished that we pulled it off. We just lived one day at a time. Our faith, **Fortitude** and love for the sacredness of family prevailed.

Missy (Stephanie)
holding Shane
Ryan in front, Brandon
The Christmas before
Missy's stroke.

Our four Grandsons
Alexander in front, back left, Shane and Ryan
Big brother Brandon in the back – 1991

Front: Shane, Ryan and Alexander
Back: A Diamond, Bill and Brandon ~ 1993
We became Grand-"Parents", Alexander is
our son,Ted's, son

161

Niece Judy with sons Justin and Daniel

Sweet Niece Judy, what would we have done without you? When Missy was so ill, you cleaned, baby-sat and even cooked. You were truly our Angel.

Thank You

Chapter 16

Guided Meditation: Humility

*To prepare yourself for this meditation please read through its
entirety. Then sit quietly and pay close attention to your breath.
Begin to read again slowly following the guidance.*

*Settling myself down, closing my eyes and taking three long deep breaths, I
am imagining my dear friend*
Sweet Humility.

Hiding from me as always, she is most shy at first.

Humility won't even poke her head out until she is absolutely sure
you are sincere about wanting to know her better.

I take three more long deep breaths and wait patiently for her to reveal herself.

Sometimes she pops up quickly and other times she needs a little
coaxing.

Sweet Humility is so childlike in her appearance;
always wearing a soft, long white dress, never wanting to call
attention to herself.

Aaah, there she is, so beautiful in her simplicity.

What she doesn't know is that it is this very modest demeanor that shines forth from her and attracts others to her.

She draws near and gently takes my hand.

Her presence conveys peace and harmony and I implore her,

"Dear Sweet Humility,

Help me to remember to invite you in often.

Help me to always look for goodness in others.

Help me to uplift and affirm others so they can feel good about themselves.

Help me to embody your tenderness and gentleness toward others."

She gently presses the tiny index fingers of her hands, one to my heart and one to her lips, encouraging silence.

We sit together quietly for a few moments.

As we take long deep breaths

She smiles and lets me know she is always with me.

I open my eyes and feel her presence,
knowing the peace and harmony will continue to sustain me throughout the day.

I Love You, My Friend Humility

Memoir: I AM Humility

If Aunt Louise said it, IT MUST BE TRUE!!! That evening after Grandma Metz's Rosary celebration, the night before her funeral Mass, Mom stopped to speak with her Aunt Louise, Grandma's eldest daughter. Sis and I sort of just hung back, not knowing what to say to Aunt Louise who was the classic picture of austerity and had the typical "Old Maid" presence: long skirt, hair in a bun, no make-up, never smiling.

My only remembrance of having interacted with her was as a kindergartner. Recalling at age five years, after my half day, morning session ending at noon, I was marched across the street, hand in hand, by my oldest brother, Steve.

Monday through Friday he took me to Grandma Metz's house, where Aunt Louise lived in the family home. We were met at the door by this tall, never smiling, slender woman. Without speaking, she led me to a small isolated room, where I was to stay, lying on a single bed until I was retrieved by Steve at 3:00 pm.

No one in this household spoke with me nor offered any kind of drink or food or stimulation. The door was closed, and I was confined to an approximately 9'x10' room. There was a twin bed, a rocker and someone's clothes hanging on a kind of makeshift closet. (I had a sense this was Uncle George's room, who I remember as a man with a crippling affliction.) There was a small window facing the street, but I never dared to leave the bed I was told to lay on to peer out. I would sometimes nap or just count the flowers on the wallpaper while waiting to be retrieved. These relatives seemed to believe the admonition,

"Children are to be seen and not heard." They fulfilled it to a tee!

Aunt Louise was my great-aunt. She and Grandma apparently had been asked to keep me, the five-year-old, in a safe place since no one was at home to look after me. Mother worked nights and had to sleep during the day but left for work by the time I was delivered home.

If this whole process seems rather robotic and stoic, as I pull it from my memory bank, that's exactly how it is remembered. Steve resented this task of delivering his little sister from place to place and my supposed "caretakers" let me know in no uncertain terms that my presence was a grand intrusion on their lives. At five years of age, I got it! I was a huge inconvenience for these after school caregivers. Mother, whom I adored, was always kind and gentle with me, but there was only so much of her to go around and she had to work full time to support us.

Never did I question any of the delivering me from place to place process, nor did I rebel. That's just the way it was, and I considered my existence to be the way it was for everyone.

Mom always spoke very highly of Aunt Louise, who I believe was very religious and attended daily Mass. In fact, her demeanor was very much like the nuns at school. She had never married and was the caregiver to her mother, Grandma Metz. Aunt Louise was the sister of Mom's father who had been shot and killed by Mom's mother, my Grandma Liz. Perhaps my last statement explains why there was such an intense sadness permeating the entire atmosphere of that three-story brick homestead across the street from St. Augustine's Church and elementary school. Maybe my presence brought up a memory of

166

an event they would rather not revisit.

Sensitive child that I was, being there left me with a very eerie feeling. Several of Great-Grandma's older children and their families shared the living spaces on the many floors. They called it a three-story brick flat.

All the rooms were kept dark. The furniture was well polished and crisp white curtains graced the tall narrow windows, much like a convent. The very air felt starched and cool. You knew for sure that every corner was well scrubbed and spotless. There was not a hint that children were welcome there.

Perhaps it was my grandfather's untimely death that was a factor in their permeating sadness and cold demeanor. It was difficult for me to fathom that Mom, who was so warm and loving, could be related to these unfortunate stoic people.

Mom never spoke of their coolness and seemed to just take for granted "that's just how they were." There was a definite sharp contrast to our living space. Our home may have been cluttered, but there was life and warmth and laughter. I don't ever remember any of these relatives visiting our home even though they lived only a block or so away.

It was many years after that "Rosary Memorial" night that Mom chose to reveal what Aunt Louise had said about me. It left me speechless, "Aunt Louise said that you have humility." Whatever the heck that meant, puzzled me to no end. How could she say this when she had probably spoken only a few words to me in my entire life?

I began trying to recall if I had some long-lost conversation with her that was totally blocked from my memory. The most I ever remembered saying to her was, "Hi, Aunt Louise"

167

accompanied by a hug, which I only gave because that is how my Mother greeted her.

Then I remembered: Bill and I and our wedding party had visited Grandma Metz briefly on our wedding day. My memory stretches to recall if there were some conversations exchanged with Aunt Louise at that time, but it escapes me.

I do recall the excitement of our wedding day and traveling approximately thirty-five or forty miles to spend maybe thirty minutes in my ninety-some- odd-years old Great-Grandma's austere home. I don't even think they offered us a place to sit, nor a drink of water. This visit was not high on my memory recall list.

That same old feeling of being unwelcome permeated the air. We had made this long trip to honor my Mother's wishes. She had said, "It is customary to visit the convalescent on your wedding day." Frankly, I had never heard of that before, but then I would do anything to fulfill my Mother's wishes.

I do remember walking to Great-Grandma Metz's bed, to which she was now confined and giving her a soft kiss. She could only smile and barely speak. I can still see the vision of this fragile, white hair twisted in a bun woman and get a feeling that in that kiss she conveyed to me a most tender love.

As I revisit that moment in time, there is a ghostly sense that I brought back to her a memory of her precious son, my Grandfather, Mom's longed-for father, for a brief second. I have a feeling that I bridged the moment when her son was abruptly taken from her and I somehow brought back his presence. Because of that minuscule moment of interaction, Great-grandma Metz is carried in my heart every day and has left an indelible mark forever.

168

Aunt Louise was witness to that sacred moment. Maybe she felt the sparks of spiritual exchange that occurred. Perhaps in that moment she interpreted my action as meekness or as she verbalized, "an act of humility." A feeling of closeness that I had never experienced before in that dark somber setting was conveyed. It's crazy because I cannot recall Grandma or Aunt Louise ever hugging or kissing me. (I hugged Aunt Louise, but she never hugged me back) not even as a child.

When I began this writing, I had no clue where the memories were going to take me. While it is not easy for me, with the astrological sign of Leo, to accept gifts, I reluctantly accept this gift that Aunt Louise generously bestowed upon me.

Because of it, I can say "I AM Humility" with just a little bit of pride! (Snicker, snicker)! I'm pretty sure you cannot describe someone as humble and in the same sentence say they have pride. To do so, would seem ludicrous. But I mean, if Aunt Louise said it, IT MUST BE TRUE!!! LOL!

Aunt Louise Metz, Mama's "Dear Aunt"

I believe this woman, though austere, provided much protective "Grace" through her prayers for our family.

Great-Great Grandma Dickman & her daughter,
Great-Grandma Anna Metz

Great Grandma, Anna Metz, & her 6 daughters
Left: Grandma, Great-Aunts: Selma, Agnes, Florence, Anna, Minnie & Louise
I include the aunts, whom I barely knew, to honor my Mother's Ancestry

171

Chapter 17

Guided Meditation: Peace

*To prepare yourself for this meditation please read through its
entirety. Then sit quietly and pay close attention to your breath.
Begin to read again slowly following the guidance.*

Closing my eyes, I connect with my breath as it gently drifts in
and out of my nasal passages.

*I take three long deep breaths allowing my abdomen to rise and fall with each
breath. Pausing, I spend a moment just being with my breath.*

My focus is now inside my Sacred Heart feeling my breath faintly
brush against the inner walls like the soft wings of the Dove of
Peace
as it spreads its wings to soar.

In my mind's eye, I watch the dove of peace soaring above
mountains and valleys which are part of the landscape in the
secret chamber within my

Sacred Heart

The dove carries an olive branch signaling its intent to bring peace
and harmony wherever it glides.

172

Pausing, I watch the Dove of Peace gliding in and out of the billowy clouds against the powder blue sky.

My awareness is that it is my breath that is the wind beneath the wings of the dove, allowing it to fly.

I will stop and reflect many times today on the dove of peace soaring in my Sacred Heart.

I AM PEACE

Memoir: I AM Peace

On that morning of March 19th, 2003, my memory carries me to having received an email from a cousin who was ecstatic and cheering. She was overjoyed. "The United States is going into Iraq to avenge the 9/11 destruction of the Trade Center and the lost lives."

My whole body began to shake and sobs began to wrack my soul. In the very core of my being I knew this was a terrible mistake. There was a slight premonition that the consequences of this action would change our lives and the lives of thousands, perhaps millions of others forever.

My anger toward the George W. Bush administration mushroomed into **intense** anger. March 19th, 2003, the date seemed to flash off and on like a neon sign. Until that day my perception of peace was beyond shallow. Early childhood memories of my Dad having been in the Second World War as a sailor and my brother, Steve had joined the Navy post second–world-war.

A very dear Uncle Ed had also been in the Army in 1944. Fortunately, it wasn't necessary to hang any "Gold Stars" in our windows, which would have signaled the loss of a loved one in that war era. Perhaps if our family had experienced a casualty, my whole perspective on war would have taken a 180-degree turn.

Then there was the Korean War, in which my-then-to be future husband had served. The Vietnam War was a source of fear that our soon-to- be eligible son, Ted, would perhaps be drafted. Yes, war was an ongoing reality throughout my early life and even into the later years, including the Granada War and the Gulf War.

Little did I suspect, our grandson, Brandon, would eventually be deployed to Iraq for this Iraqi War. During Brandon's deployment, Bill and I could barely hold back tears every time we saw a soldier on the street. We found ourselves going up and thanking them for their service, somehow feeling like in doing so we were a little closer to Brandon.

As a child, there was a conscious sadness within when seeing the newsreels of the wars in the movies, but nothing rocked me like that Iraqi War. I could envision the world's mothers and fathers weeping and whaling at the loss of their precious sons and daughters.

Were our leaders blind and deaf to the pain and agony their decision to invade Iraq would reap? Why couldn't they see that vengeance was not the way? Peace had to be pursued until there was not a single word left to be said, until the tear-soaked cloths from previous wars had been wrung bone dry.

The sadness of that moment carried me back to a time when I was seven years old standing with a same-age, distant cousin, Annette. We were outside a huge brick and stone, high-steeple church. Having been ushered from the gathering by our Aunt Rose, we could still hear the sobs and unbearable whaling of the relatives within. This was Annette's daddy's funeral and Aunt Rose was trying to protect us from the sadness that permeated the very walls of that cavernous citadel. This still-young man had been killed in action, which I now believe was called The Normandy Invasion.

While Aunt Rose's intervention was partially effective, the overwhelming insufferable darkness that permeated the air crept silently from beneath the massive, tall wooden doors into my bones. Those moments are frozen in time.

I can still remember the color and texture of little Annette's beige, woolen, camel-hair coat, which she pulled around her legs to protect herself from the harsh Midwestern winter wind. Her soft blonde hair was long in back and braided in front, gently framing her sweet pink, frost-bitten cheeks creating contrast with the rest of her starkly pale face.

Annette wasn't crying, as I recall. It's as if she was in shock. I often wonder if she remembers those moments so vividly as I do. Having to leave his precious, small daughter by being killed in a far- away land was beyond comprehension for our young, still-trusting minds.

Those moments solidified my distaste for the process of solving disputes by waging war. Though Annette and I never really had interaction after that memorable day, I still carry her in my heart.

On that momentous day in 2003, as I reread the email from my cousin, my response was short and swift. My thoughts were, "No need to relay to her the sorrow her message had dug up from the grave of my sad memories." All I could type was *PEACE, PEACE, PEACE at any price*! To which there was never another response from my cousin. It was as if the years of our corresponding and connection had been irreparably severed. In truth, I wanted to take her and shake her to awaken her to the horrors that war visits upon us.

In that moment all the sweet memories of her and I

176

together melted away and I was left with a void of thinking, "I don't even know this person if we don't have this resolve for peace in common." The words "invasion and war" were not even a part of my consciousness, much less welcomed in my vocabulary.

For me "war" conjures up another dreaded picture of a close friend's son, Dennis Young, who was incinerated in a tank in the Vietnam War. He was just in his early twenties. This loss shook our whole family in disbelief that someone so vital could just be taken in an instant. It made no sense.

As I reflect now, I believe that unless someone is touched to the core by the pain of war, they cannot understand how ingrained the aversion becomes in one's psyche. When someone crosses the line that offends you to the core, little can breach the chasm. I had to consciously choose to try and look at the situation from my cousin's perspective. My conclusion was that the horrible 9/11 tragedy had cut her so deeply that it caused her to be able to rationalize that taking other lives in vengeance was 'just' compensation. I knew the sweetness that she truly was at her core. Her response blinded me to all those gentle memories of her.

I had to draw back and take my judgment out of the equation of our relationship. "Lest we walk a mile in another's shoes we cannot know their motives." goes the saying.

All I know is that for me, nothing can justify taking another's life. So many scripture verses allude to how we are to act as human beings. "Vengeance is mine", says the Lord. Romans 12:19. "When someone offends you, turn the other cheek." Matthew 5:38-40 "Love your neighbor as yourself." Mark 12:3. Pretty self-righteous of me, right?

I have a sense that these statements were uttered by someone who knew the pain of losing a loved one. This had to be someone who knew this outrageous advice could not be easily incorporated into our belief system of "an eye for an eye." This person is advising us to override the status quo, "bite the bullet" and reach for a higher vibrational standard. "When they go low, we go high", said Michelle Obama.

Peace and promoting good health were part of my everyday life as I coordinated the Reunion Holistic Health Center in Pleasant Hill, CA from 1993 until 2007. Pathways Health and Peace Center became my focus from 2007 to date, 2018. For many years, several of us coordinated a Sunday Service called "Pathways To Peace." Peace has become my mantra. I even end writings with "Sent in Peace."

If you haven't read the book RADICAL FORGIVENESS by Colin Tipping, now may be the perfect time. In this magnificent book, Colin presents a formula or method he has developed and shared across the entire U.S. in seminars. I had the privilege of meeting Colin when he offered his seminar at our Center.

Through using these principles and the ritual recommended, I found I was able to let go of a deep anger for someone who had injured our whole family with repeated behaviors that caused us almost daily injury and sadness.

Once I was able to replace my wounds and anger with compassion, as advised in Colin's book (it doesn't come easily) that "Peace that passes understanding" Philippians 4:7 began to seep into my whole being. In fact, this person that I held in anger, came to our door and offered an apology and asked for forgiveness.

It was a miracle. One that I will never forget. By letting go of my attitude toward this person, it literally changed a vibration I had been holding them in. I became totally convinced that PEACE is really the flip side of a coin called anger and vengeance.

I continue my mantra:

I AM

PEACE, PEACE, PEACE

Dennis Young ~ A Dear Friend of our family.
He gave his life in Vietnam at the age of 21 years.

"We have loved them during life, .
let us not forget them in death."
St. Ambrose

IN LOVING MEMORY OF

Pfc. Dennis Lee Young
U. S. Army
August 3, 1949
April 2, 1970

180

Bill's Dad, Joseph Trammel ~ 1918
First World War
A Quiet Peaceful Man

Edmond & Stephan Tamborski
2nd World War
Uncle Ed & Daddy, Brothers ~ 1944

Wally Press (Paw-Paw Wally)
Momma's 2nd husband

182

Commander Joseph Winston
Trammel Airforce 1942
Bill's Brother, Fighter Pilot
Instructor

Bill ~ Airforce 1952
We wrote many love letters to one another.
I was just 15 and Bill was 20.

183

My brother Steve
Tamborski ~ 1949

Grandson Brandon Wilson ~ 2005
Deployed to Iraq

Great-Nephew Daniel Bradbury – 2005
Deployed to Iraq

185

Honorable Mention:

Bill's brothers:
John Trammel, 2nd World War
Served in Japan
Harold Trammel, Korean War

Cousin:
Frank Tamborski, 2nd World War
Served in Holland

Nephew
Jerry Reposa
Served in Vietnam

While pictures of the above men in uniform were not available, we do want to honor them for their service.

Chapter 18

Guided Meditation: Laughter

*To prepare yourself for this meditation please read through its
entirety. Then sit quietly and pay close attention to your breath.
Begin to read again slowly following the guidance.*

The angels sing and the earth is set back on its course
by the sound of laughter

With the above statement resounding in my heart,

I close my eyes and take three long deep breaths.

I cannot wait to enter the sanctuary of my Sacred Heart
to find the surprise that will elicit the joy
that spontaneously bursts forth into laughter.

In my heart's eye, I see children running and squealing.

They have stumbled upon a precious puppy who is entertaining
them
with its antics and cute somersaults.

The puppy has discovered its tail and is chasing it round and
round.

It rolls on its back and tries every conceivable position to reach its

187

own extremity to no avail.

pausing I take three long deep breaths

Puppy hops like a bunny as it is distracted and surprised by its shadow.

Oh, now it's a grasshopper that is capturing its attention and puppy stalks it and pounces only to discover Mr. Grasshopper has outsmarted him.

The sounds of the children's laughter explodes in my Sacred Heart
and spills over into all the cells of my body,
bringing healing endorphins and magical elixirs that boost my immune system.

Laughter is, truly, the best medicine.

Today, I will find time in the quietness of my own private space to
LAUGH OUT LOUD
and feel the joy of my inner child.

I pause and take three long deep breaths

As I open my eyes, I make a commitment to recall the times when
I have laughed big belly laughs
and remind myself, that:

I AM LAUGHTER

Memoir: I Am Laughter

"Laugh! Laugh often, long and loud. Laugh until you gasp for breath. Shared laughter creates a bond of friendship." Author unknown

There we were, two grown women, me in my sixties, Alexis Summerfield in her fifties, lying on the ground at the Lafayette Bart Station. Gasping for air, we were laughing so hard. Whatever sparked that uncontrollable eruption, which began on the Bart train, has long been forgotten. However, the bond it created is unforgettable.

At our stop, we had to, literally, fall out the doors with our huge shopping bags and drag ourselves away from the opening. My dear friend and I were like two school kids lost in our own magical moment in time. This is still a truly cherished memory.

One of my dearest clients and friend, Kathryn DeSilva, gave me a plaque with the above quote that I have hung in my Holistic Health Center. She knew I would appreciate it since I use the technique of laughter in my spiritual counseling practice quite often. It is one of the best ways I know to help a person to "let go" and relax. Clients, the first time they hear me being able to "belly laugh" spontaneously and without reserve in order to encourage them to laugh, are usually taken by surprise and respond by belly laughing aloud themselves.

Recalling moments of uncontrollable laughter come crashing in like ocean waves exploding on the face of sentinel rocks protecting the fragile coastline. Discerning which to share

189

here without bombarding and boring you with an endless parade of comical events, one that caused me the most embarrassment seems appropriate.

Dolores Moynihan was one of my closest friends and had invited me to attend her high school as a guest student. It all started off quite innocently. However, Dolores was one of my combustible laughter triggers. She and I had experienced many spastic laughing sessions on various occasions. I guess that is why we were such close friends.

Once one of us started laughing, the infectious laughter could go on for what seemed like eternity. Well...this is what happened in Mr. Wood's science class when I was a guest. It did not end well. I was invited to leave the school and Dolores was sent to the principal's office. If you can believe it, throughout the entire process, both of us continued to laugh. The worst part of it was that Mr. Wood was my science teacher the following year. The embarrassment was a continuous thorn in my side for many classes that year.

While I have trained myself to laugh aloud with abandonment that is a laugh, I am able to turn off and on. I'm not sure if this is true for everyone but for me there are certain people who, when we are together begin our spontaneous laughter, we cannot stop: My Mom, my sister, a childhood friend, Dolores, Alexis, our daughter, Stephanie, my nieces, Denise and Micki and also a great-niece, Lisa and perhaps a few more are my triggers. Somehow there is a kind of chemistry that we feed on from one another that allows us to ignite a spark that becomes a raging wildfire. Our laughter is like spontaneous combustion and we fuel one another's wild blaze until it becomes uncontrollable

190

and spreads like an inferno.

I'm sure there have been more than a few times when other people would have liked to have stuffed a towel in our mouths or put a bag over our heads, which of course would have only made us laugh longer and louder. Some kids never grow up!

To share just a few of the treasured times that can still make my heart almost burst with joy: Our family had taken a trip to Tahoe and my Sis and I laid in the back of the station wagon with our feet hanging out the back (before seat belts). We laughed until we were almost sick all the way back home. (Not sure why.)

I believe this was also the time our Mom had come from the ladies' room with toilet paper stuck to her shoe and she was dragging it behind her. Mom, Sis and I laughed uncontrollably over and over every time one of us thought about it. One of my cousins once said, "I just love to hear Aunt Mickey laugh, (my Mom) she makes everybody laugh."

Then there was the time our niece Denise, and I were on Bart (Bay Area Rapid Transit) heading for the airport to celebrate my and Bill's 50th Wedding anniversary in Hawaii. Bill cautioned us to "hold on!" Denise and I both grabbed our luggage handles and when the train started up, we fell on top of one another and that contagious infectious laughter began and didn't subside for most of the trip.

And then of course I can always count on a laughter fix since our daughter, Stephanie, lives with us and we have our ecstatic laughing moments on a regular basis. I Don't want to leave out the time great-niece Lisa and I created a scenario together that was fed by the way a lady was dancing at our nephew Steven's party. We both tried to tell our husbands why we were so profusely laughing, but we couldn't even talk sensibly between gasps for breath.

Laughing aloud by myself, in my car, when something stressful is challenging me really allows me to see the situation in a different perspective. I have heard it is recommended that everyone needs to laugh aloud several times a day for their health.

When our daughter, Sylvia, worked in the corporate world, her company sent their work force to a one-day seminar in which they were taught to laugh spontaneously, daily, to counteract taking sick days. It was called a "Laughter Workshop." The other purpose was to teach the employees to "lighten up."

It is my understanding that when we laugh out loud our brain has no way of telling if we just heard or saw something hilarious or if we are just self-stimulating and responds by prompting our body to produce endorphins, which are natural tranquilizers. Apparently, it is the sound we produce that triggers the response.

In my spiritual counseling practice, I use Reiki, Aura Cleansing and Chakra Balancing. Each of the seven Chakras has a different tone or sound. Laughter is the sound for the throat Chakra. When a person is going through depression, no matter the cause, learning to laugh on a regular basis is one of the most beneficial treatments they can adopt for themselves. Laughter costs nothing and has no detrimental side-effects.

I highly recommend the practice of laughing aloud at least three times each day. That's why it has been said: **Laughter Really Is The Best Medicine.**

Following are many of the people that have laughed "convulsively" with me on many occasions. What a blast it would be if we could all be present at a party at the same time.

Great-Niece, Lisa Jones

Her laughter is infectious

Our beautiful daughter Stephanie, 2006

Living with her allows Bill and I to have our dose of belly laughs almost every day

Niece Denise
No one loves a party more ~ A heart of pure gold

Grandson Brandon and his beautiful wife, Danielle

When they come to visit and we play games our contagious laughter rules the day.

Alexis Sumerfield

Who knows if I would have ever entered the Metaphysical World without prompting from Alexis

We fell out of Bart laughing convulsively

Niece Micki Rodrigues
She was named after her grandmother, my mother.
She also inherited Mom's great
sense of humor, par-excellence.

Chapter 19

Guided Meditation: Forgiveness

*To prepare yourself for this meditation please read through its
entirety. Then sit quietly and pay close attention to your breath.
Begin to read again slowly following the guidance.*

Today, I will practice Forgiveness toward myself for all the times I
have not fulfilled my promises and extended Forgiveness to
anyone who I perceive has harmed or wounded me.

As I make this statement I can see

Divine Mother and Father

seated inside the doorway of my Sacred Heart, welcoming me in
with open arms.

With my eyes closed and pausing,

I take three long deep breaths and exhale slowly

to allow this magical vision to soak deeply into my imagination.

The ultraviolet light of Forgiveness streams out of the doorway,
enveloping my Divine Parents and flowing toward me, wrapping
my spirit in the warm soft blanket of unconditional love.

I can feel their Divine hugs loving me back into oneness with them.

They invite me to sit between them.

We hold hands for several minutes, basking in the knowing that I myself have been forgiven for any of my failings,

past, present and future.

I take three long deep breaths and exhale slowly

I am prompted to stand and walk slowly back to the doorway of my Sacred Heart and send the ultraviolet light of love to all those whom I perceive have harmed me in this life and in the past.

They begin to appear and I am welcoming them, one by one, offering my own

Divine Hug.

Healing ultraviolet light continues to flow from my heart into the river of life in my body, bringing the light and life of Forgiveness into every cell of my being.

Focusing on my breath, I open my eyes and feel the freedom of this transformation.

My soul is at peace as I repeat three times:

I AM FORGIVENESS,

I AM FORGIVEMESS, I AM FORGIVENESS

Memoir: I AM Forgiveness

What??? That's a bit much to ask of any human to *"forgive seventy times seven"*, Matt. 18:22. If only I had allowed that verse to take root in my heart and grow, many years of anguish could have been avoided. If you have ever lived any length of time in the state of not forgiving, you may be acutely aware of how much unrest this creates in your entire being.

Speaking as an authority on this subject, it took me many years to understand what was being stated in that scripture verse "do whatever it takes to allow yourself to be at peace...even if it takes that many times seventy times seven to achieve it." It is with much conviction that I say, forgive or be willing to suffer the consequences.

More and more, I am convinced that this man, Jesus, had a profound grasp on the human condition. However, he recognized the need to present his message in a way to appeal to the mentality of the age in which he found himself. *"I have come that they may have life; that they may have it more abundantly."* John 10:10.

With no intention to proselytize or to convince anyone of my spiritual beliefs, I share this only to present my experience with the hope it may help someone to avoid the pain and anguish I put myself through. By not believing in the power of forgiveness, nor incorporating it into my life for a long period of time, the consequences became life threatening and certainly life altering.

A little history leading up to my unbending expectations: At age seventeen, my preconceived idea of what a happy, successful marriage looked like was definitely not anything close to what had been demonstrated in my parent's marriage. Searching for the magic formula, my Dad's sister, Aunt Helen and her husband, Uncle Frank, seemed the closest I could discern to be the ideal union. Their picture: Three beautiful, well-behaved daughters, a stay-at-home mom, their own small cottage style home complete with white picket fence. What more could anyone ask?

Marrying at a young age (seventeen years) was the accepted norm in the Midwest during the nineteen-fifties. Bill had been on my radar since I was ten years old. He was my brother Rich's best friend and our close neighbor. We had similar backgrounds; living in postwar military housing in a place called Jefferson Barracks in South St. Louis County, Missouri. We were, also, of the approximate same economic status.

Of course, Bill, being five years my senior, had no idea how impressed I was with his mannerisms. Wow!! I really thought he was good looking. I wrote undelivered love letters to him on several occasions that lay lost and forgotten in my old chest of drawers. These notes were not remembered or recovered until the day after our wedding while clearing out my old chest. I was startled, but pleasantly surprised, when they fell onto the floor. They had been hiding behind the drawer and revealed themselves when I removed it.

People speak of having met their "soul mates." I had never heard this term in my early years, but many years later upon hearing it expressed, I was totally convinced this was true of our relationship. In fact, after becoming one of the coordinators of a Holistic Health Center in 1993, I had the opportunity to do many "past-life regressions" that helped me understand numerous events in my life. It is my definite belief that we had been around the block together in another lifetime.

On the morning of our wedding, the priest required that I attend 6:30 am Mass. Bill was not Catholic so there could be no Mass during our ceremony, and we could not receive communion. After Mass, I lingered and spent time in the presence of the Mother Mary statue asking a special blessing on our marriage and that Bill and I would have a happy life together.

In addition, after our wedding ceremony, before exiting the church as part of our wedding ritual, I placed a bouquet of white carnations at the foot of the statue of the Blessed Mother and gave her a wink. For me, it was like making a sacred contract with her trusting that her presence would always be felt guiding us on our wedded path.

I was terrified to consider repeating the horror story of my Mom and Dad's nuptials. Infidelity, rage, abuse, violence, unkempt promises, Making-up, breaking-up, a nightmare of events was the model I had witnessed. Having a happy marriage was the most essential requisite for me to make my life have meaning.

For most of my early life all I could wish for was to have a baby. I never really wanted a husband or any man in my life. Quite a far cry from what the seventeen-year-old Audrey, was signing up for and requiring of her marriage. My suspicion is that my love for children was acquired by osmosis from my Mother. It was no secret that her children were her sole reason for living. Most naturally, I concluded babies and children were the beginning and the end of all that had meaning and importance.

OMG, my darling Bill, little did he know the intensity to which he would be subjected since I was barely in touch with all these extreme feelings and prerequisites myself. He was, and is, without a doubt, the most patient, understanding person I have ever had the pleasure of knowing. Over the years, the expression, "If I ever did anything right, it was to marry Bill", found its way to my lips.

I said it then and I can still say it is true today, "A man never stands so tall as when he stoops to tie a little child's shoe." This quote epitomizes the profile of my dear husband, Bill.

Having come from a family with simple, uncomplicated values, country folk, Bill was 180 degrees away from what I had known of the men in my family. I am so grateful to whoever directed my life journey for allowing our paths to cross. For the first time in my life I had discovered a man I could trust and love wholeheartedly.

It is important for me to describe to you the emotional investment I had made into our marriage in order to help you understand the depth of despair I felt when Bill and I met our greatest marriage challenge. You might say "I had put all my eggs in one basket." No one person should ever be expected to live on the precarious pedestal to which Bill had been elevated. I had set myself up for him to have a fall that could only be cushioned by my intense pride; the kind of perverse pride that gives birth to arrogance and the intent for revenge.

At first my inclination was not to disclose any of the particulars of this dark time of our lives and to only share the rupture that was created. I soon realized that to allow a reader to draw their own conclusions would unjustly allow them to take our "divine tragedy" anywhere their imagination could take it. Therefore, in all fairness to the man I love, I must convey the exact nature of what occurred.

Almost ten years into our wedded bliss, Bill became a police officer for St. Louis County. Thank you God/Goddess. At that time this was a sane, and certainly not tumultuous place for him to work. Traffic stops, petty burglaries, unacceptable drunkenness in public, domestic violence were probably the most serious crimes to which he was confronted. None of the shootings that we hear of today existed back in those times.

When a position on the Narcotics Squad was up for bid, Bill saw it as a promotion and chose to try for it. I mean, when I look back, this was ludicrous. Bill was not a drinker and what was required was to act like a casual customer and catch tavern owners or bartenders selling illegal drinks.

St Louis County is considered a part of the Bible Belt and, at the time, there were "Blue Laws", meaning no hard-alcoholic drinks could be sold after certain hours or on Sundays. In the process of his assignments, he had to work evenings and patronize the night spots, consuming a certain amount of alcohol as a regular customer. When someone was spotted being served an illegal drink, a warning or an arrest was made. Sounds simple enough!

However, to make it all seem more authentic and believable, unbeknownst to me, the undercover officers often had a female accompany them. Bill's narcotic's officer assignment was short lived when I discovered the name and phone number of a woman, in his suit pocket when preparing to send his suit to the cleaners.

Shortly after, the full story was unveiled. A time bomb was triggered within me and all the mistrust of men, which I had displaced in our relationship, erupted. "Never underestimate the wrath of a woman scorned."

I called the woman and met with her to discover that, yes, she was falling in love with my husband although their relationship had not progressed to the intimate stage. To this day, I am not sure what my response would have been if the situation had been otherwise. Crazy with rage, all the pent-up fear and anger over what my most dreaded nightmares were about now wanted to erupt and cause an explosion.

I am ashamed to admit that Grandma Liz's solution to infidelity crossed my mind (Grandma had shot and killed our grandfather over infidelity, hers not his). All my insecurities were exposed to the raw cold of the subzero temperature of those Midwestern winter nights.

My recalling the nights I spent praying Bill would be safe as a narcotics officer, out in the cold, while our three small children and I slumbered in our warm cozy beds, smacked me in the face. That dark side of my psyche was shouting, *what a fool you have been to ever trust any man*! I believe my distrust of men had been encoded on my "super-neural-highways" a term I later discovered in reading the book "One Spirit Medicine by Alberto Villoldo. (pg 27) I didn't understand it at the time, but the following explains for me why I felt this betrayal to the depth of my soul. I let it take me to my depths.

"It is believed that as many as half of our neural maps of reality are formed in the womb, as the mother's stress

204

hormones pass through the placental barrier to the fetus. So if your mother was not sure she could count on your father to be there and support her, your map will code for a reality in which you can't count on men to be there for you or a universe where men will not support your endeavors."

GET IT?

This was my most NIGHTMARISH FEAR; the fear of infidelity that I had integrated into my very bones. The fear from which I believed I would not be able to survive. My senses told me, *if you don't act fast this fear has the power to send you to the depths of despair.*

My instincts kicked in and I went into survival mode to protect myself and our children. I closed my heart that night and put an iron fence around it. That very night I called my Mom who had moved to California after the death of her husband, Bill Rich. Without much explanation I conveyed to her "The children and I will be boarding a plane in the morning. Please have one of my brothers meet me at the airport." Knowing the dark side of my nature, which I had only rarely shown to anyone, it was best that I get as far away from this situation as possible. Although deep in my heart I knew that what had happened was not really who Bill was, the irrational side of me pushed any reasoning aside.

Initially, my stubborn side refused to allow me to return Bill's numerous phone calls. Finally, I relented. As I came to my senses, spending only one week away from Bill, my life was miserable. It didn't take me long to realize all the dreams we had built upon were too solid and valuable to throw away. We communicated by phone often as I prepared to return to our home.

205

Bill put in his resignation as narcotics officer and returned to the position of patrol officer and though we tried to resume our regular lives, for me, I knew it could never be the same. Bill's brother, Harold, on consoling Bill, in my absence, said it so precisely, "What happened is that you broke a sacred trust." Couldn't have said it better myself!

While my words said "I forgive you," my heart had built an armor around it and I made a conscious decision to never love and trust that deeply again.

I kept the wound well hidden, but it festered inside like a boil, wanting to wreak havoc but never wanting to do injury to our children. It is sheer craziness that allowed a person, me, to function and continue to bury a wound so deep it seemed to become an extra appendage or organ that began to feel necessary in order to survive.

Now I can only hope our children were not drastically affected by the covert wound I kept wrapped in not forgiving. Knowing all things are relevant, I am sure my interactions with everyone had to be colored by my internal turmoil. I became guarded and suspicious of any new friends we met.

The immature religious practices, which I mistook for deep faith came into question. At that time, I had no awareness that sometimes deeper faith and religious beliefs don't keep pace with one another. In childish expectations, I felt betrayed by God himself. Still using my religion as a kind of insurance policy, *as long as I paid the premiums, praying and attending Mass, I felt deserving of protection from the disasters of my greatest fears.* I asked myself, *Hey, what about the contract I had made with Mother Mary on my wedding day?*

Not forgiving created within me two people. One wanting

to lash out and return "an eye for an eye" and the other not daring to destroy the beauty of what Bill and I had created together. I knew I could never find another man who would love our children as he did.

With an intent to save our marriage, we made our trek from the Midwest to California to start anew. Mom and my brothers had moved to California several years before and we were invited to share housing with Mom until we could get settled.

California was the new frontier I needed to distract myself from my preoccupation with our near disaster. We were not able to get our son, Ted, age nine years, into parochial school, which he had attended previously. This was a great disappointment since both Bill, and I valued the religious training along with the academics the private school offered.

St. Agnes Church opened a new school as our girls were becoming of age and we were able to register them for classes. The old kind of overbearing discipline and strict doctrines had been greatly relaxed by the Ecumenical Council. I felt they were safe from the stern, heavy hands of the nuns I had experienced.

Life by all outward appearances returned to normalcy. Bill and I both worked in order to achieve and maintain the standard of living we desired for ourselves and our children. Ted, Stephanie (Missy) and Sylvia thrived in the sunny California climate and the closeness of family and cousins, it gave them a sense of tribe and belonging.

As the children grew, a restlessness began to well up within me. Looking back now, I believe it was that lost, deep spiritual relationship pushing up the unresolved matter of not forgiving. In response, I completed my GED and chose to attend the local junior college with the goal of going into nursing. This was a vocation that seemed compatible with my natural gift of caregiving and wanting to nurture.

In the curriculum of my English class, an assignment triggered all the pain and anguish I had been harboring deep in the crevices of my soul. The task of writing my autobiography opened the floodgates holding back all the memories. All the sediment and pain of the previous eight years forced me to take a look at the ugly sewage I had allowed to accumulate due to my inability to forgive.

My nervous system felt very fragile and I recognized a need to reconnect with my spiritual roots. One morning after a prayer time in our garden, I picked up an English walnut which had fallen from our tree. It looked perfect and shiny on the outside. That inner voice, which had guided me so many times in the past, whispered in my ear, *Open the walnut.* Using my fingers to separate the shell, I almost wanted to scream as I dropped its contents, reviled at what I found. Inside was a rotten nutmeat being devoured by worms. Repulsed, I backed away from the site as my inner voice *said, "This is what has become of your beautiful faith. It has shriveled and died. As you begin to rebuild your belief system, you will grow a new shoot from the root and it will be stronger and bear new fruit."* I knew these words were true; I had read them in scripture before. Isaiah 11:1

Devastated and sobbing, I became acutely aware of how far I had fallen from the grace of all my former high ideals. Pride and non-forgiveness had taken me down a path to diminished health and a loss of all I valued and held dear.

At age thirty-five, I was feeling very old and spent. Non-forgiveness had taken all my vitality and strength. Keeping up the charade was no longer possible. It was time to take a good look at myself and get honest.

Doctors had previously stated in some of my readings, "There is no such thing as a nervous breakdown." I beg to differ with them. Only someone who has suffered such an intense breakdown of their entire nervous system can testify and challenge their conclusions. When a strong multitasking, totally capable woman, such as I was, is reduced to a pathetically dependent person, incapable of boiling water or choosing which clothes to wear, shaking inside and crying uncontrollably, I define that malady as a "nervous breakdown."

At the time I experienced the deepest conceivable state of depression that I now contribute to my not choosing to forgive. My strong facade of hiding un-forgiveness collapsed allowing me to recapture the true nature of my being. It took me well over a year to totally recuperate after having to be hospitalized and I still cherish this event as one of the greatest blessings of my life.

I had an inner knowing that had I not let my guard down, surrendered and allowed forgiveness to come in and set up residence, the entire course of my life would have gone downhill. My life path was intended to be one of spiritual awareness and service to others. That is what has always made my heart sing. *"Follow your bliss and the universe will open doors for you where there were only walls." Joseph* Campbell.

Living without the fullness of love and trust stunted my spiritual growth and affected my physical health. Without Bill's unconditional love and being there every step of the way, I may not have made it. He nurtured me back to health and was there for our children when I was not able.

Telling Bill how I had harbored a desire to give him a wound equal to mine prompted him to take me in his arms and say while sobbing, "If I could take you to the highest mountain away from all that hurt, I would." In that instant, healing flooded into my heart and I knew that after eight years of tormenting and not forgiving, my confession and willingness to forgive would ensure us a good life together for many, many years to come.

I risk writing this account in the hope that if I can save one single person the agony and pain of not forgiving, it is worth it. My error was that my pride would not allow me to show my true feelings and how vulnerable and fragile I felt.

The false facade of "strong woman" which I wanted to present to my family and friends was put before my good health and sense of well-being. My wonderful husband and children were, I believe, robbed of many hours of joy and happiness when I could not fully show how much they were treasured and loved.

Forgiving seventy times seven may seem over the top, but if you break it down, it would have been 490 days I needed to admit I was having a difficult time forgiving. Instead, I spent eight years (2,920 days) of agony and unrest as a trade-off.

My account may sound rather fundamental and literal. I am trying to create a visual aid to bring home the fact that whatever it takes, forgiveness is the only route. There is a friend in my life who is now severely mentally ill. She has spent the last thirty years of her life hating her ex-husband and not being able to forgive him his infidelity. There is a strong correlation in my mind that her choosing anger and resentment over forgiveness has been a huge factor in her illness.

Sometimes a person is not worthy of your trust and you may have to exit from that relationship. The main issue is to beware that not forgiving can pollute the rest of your life. It hurts you, not them.

Watching the downward spiral of my dear Mother's life, there is no doubt in my mind that her unwillingness to forgive my Father for all his abuse wounded her ten times more than it did him. Not forgiving caused her to break down and changed her from the lighthearted, fun-loving beautiful woman that we had all known into a cynical, judgmental person.

As a health consultant and Reiki Practitioner (energy therapist) and Spiritual Counselor, I am often in the position to detect that not forgiving is at the root of some of my clients' ailments. I have been able to help them to let go of the anger and resentfulness that has been holding them captive.

Not forgiving benefits no one's best interest. It is my belief it creates damaging chemicals within the physical body. In the early stages, it seems to serve a purpose to cushion and protect a person from falling apart. However, not forgiving becomes an addictive drug and depletes the adrenals until a person is finally unable to cope with life itself.

Of the people I have observed with some of the mental challenges showing up: dementia, Alzheimer's, etc., my educated guess would be that the root cause started with not forgiving. In the final stages, it manifests in ways that medical doctors are trying to manage with tranquilizing pharmaceuticals that only mask the deep feelings at the base.

My best advice is this: if you or anyone you know is suffering from the disease of not forgiving (I do call it a disease) pray for divine intervention to help with this addiction. That is what I had to do. I did not have the ability to do it on my own. Not being able to forgive kills the spirit within as surely as poison kills the physical body. Choosing peace and tranquility above anger, resentfulness and revenge is highly recommended. Revenge is not sweet. It is a killer!

Forgive 70 X 7

Uncle Frank and Aunt Helen Nischbach
(Daddy's youngest Sister)
They were my role models for a "Perfect Marriage"

They had three daughters:
"Little" Helen, Francine & Mary Anne

They were life partners. Aunt Helen stayed home to raise the children and wore aprons when she cooked. They lived in a house with a white picket fence.

I thought that was all it took.

213

From a Lump of Coal to A Diamond

Our 50th Anniversary Invitation - January 22, 2005

Through 50 years our Family Treasures

Below: Pictures from our
50th Anniversary Celebration

Daughter-in-Law Deb &
Son Ted

Daughter Missy, Grandson Brandon
Wilson, Daughter Sylvia

Niece Denise Reposa &
Grandson Ryan Wilson

Jeremiah Allen
~ We had to put some of
those hombres in Jail

216

So blessed to have my three siblings and their spouses to celebrate with us.

Bill & Me, We danced to a great Country Western Band

Top: Niece Patsy Rahn, Nephew RonFry,
Nephew Greg Rahn & Grandson Brandon
Middle: Grandsons Brandon & Alexander
Bottom: Niece Debbie Fry, Sister Sis and
Brother-In-Law Dan

Lucky us to have so many friends!

Top: Nephew & Niece, Rich & Wife
Denise Tamborski &
Niece Denise Reposa
Middle and bottom: Many friends from
the Center

Eileen entertained us with her Irish Dancing

Eileen Johnston

Chapter 20

Guided Meditation: Sweet Inspiration

To prepare yourself for this meditation please read through its entirety. Then sit quietly and pay close attention to your breath. Begin to read again slowly following the guidance.

With my eyes closed, I take three long deep breaths.
You, Sweet Inspiration are so innately interconnected with the life force energy flowing through my body.
You entice me to become aware that I am one with creation from the micro to the macro and all that exists between.
Ripples of your strength surge through me.
I pause and take three more long deep breaths.
As I gaze upon this White Diamond Crystal Light above my head it directs me to go to a deeper silence and down into my Sacred Heart
The silence forges a pathway and begins to lift my Sacred Heart until it becomes lodged in my third eye.
The two begin to communicate telepathically. I remain silent

while breathing deeply for the next few minutes. I am totally fixated and captivated by the vision of sacred knowing being transferred from my third eye into my Sacred Heart.

There are no words to convey the message of understanding these two are able to transmit to one another. My Sacred Heart is being instilled with pure

Sweet Inspiration.

I can sense it flowing into all my bodily cells

I pause and take three more long deep breaths and allow

Sweet Inspiration and my Sacred Heart

To drift down into their resting place.

Becoming more conscious of my breath, I begin to expand my Sacred Heart.

The Eternal White Diamond Crystal Light slowly drifts back to its position above my head.

Opening my eyes, I can feel the warmth as my body continues to be filled with

Sweet Inspiration

Memoir: I Am Sweet Inspiration

Despite wishing I had planted those daffodil bulbs last fall, my spirit was not dampened by my self-reproach. In fact, reproach was no match at all for the golden splendor that was presented as I enjoyed the ride along California State Highway 121 towards the town of Winters.

With each blink of my eye, I candidly snapped a permanent picture in my mind of the beauty and profusion of yellow daffodils trumpeting the first messages of spring.

Many clumped together as they leaned on one another for support, like well-acquainted family members whose clan and ancestry stretched back many generations. Others bravely stood out alone, enjoying the spirit of individual freedom and stretching their faces to the fullness of the sun.

Gratitude filled me and was directed toward that industrious gardener who had not procrastinated when the small window of "bulb planting time" arrived many fall seasons prior. I thanked them in my mind and heart for providing this grandiose floral display. There are few flowers that trigger in me such mega doses of inspiration.

Next to the fragrant gardenias or roses of summer, daffodils are my third most favorite flower. They are the first sign of spring, heralding all is well and another season is on its way with the promise of new life, growth and abundance. It seems to me that most everyone gets a sense of well-being as the spring breezes begin to blow away the residue of last winter's ashes. We can look forward to the gentle rains that soften the earth's face, allowing the tender shoots of greenery to poke through its nostrils and breathe in the glory of all that is good.

The golden yellow daffodils encourage me to reflect on some of the wondrous gifts of creation like the sand on the beach or the fruitless mulberry trees that seem to have been placed here for the sole purpose of inspiring us with their beauty. They provide a kind of billboard preview for the coming attractions we can expect from the warm sunny days of summer.

Aaah! Sweet inspiration. Without it, little of importance would be accomplished. The world would be a much lesser place in which to dwell. Inspiration is the stimuli that has motivated the great artists, poets, authors, lovers, inventors and scientists to manifest their most divine ideas and visions. Inventors and artists; da Vinci, Michelangelo and Tesla all shared they had been inspired by a divine vision, which motivated their genius.

Inspiration gives us permission to explore a limitless world and causes our heart and our breath to expand and gives us fodder to dream new dreams we never dared to imagine. It triggers virtuous responses such as love, joy, generosity, patience, kindness, forgiveness, honesty, humility and so many more. Inspiration breaks down barriers, fosters courage and empowers us to accomplish feats we once thought beyond our capabilities.

When I am being confronted with a challenge that requires me to stretch my self-imposed limitations, I list my gifts and talents on paper. I then spend time looking within each item on the list and rediscover what it was that originally inspired me to develop a skill or to expand a God/Goddess- given talent. I ask myself, "Did this particular trait originate from love, a person, place, book, event, painting, movie, etc.?" When I begin to determine the inspiration behind each one of those abilities, a new understanding and insight into what inspires me to reach for the stars is revealed. The author Catherine Ponder once said, "If you reach for the stars, you will never come up with a handful of mud."

To cite an example of inspiration: Many years ago, in St. Louis, Missouri (when I was an occasional delivery person for a pharmacy in my mid-twenties), my delivery route included mostly elderly people who were no longer driving. That day I knocked on the door of one of our elderly customers. She did not answer the door but called to me, "Come in." The scene which was presented has inspired me hundreds of times over the years. There on the floor was this stately, eightyish-year-old woman doing her exercises. She did not want to stop and so had me leave the delivery on the table, informing me that she allowed nothing to interrupt her daily exercises.

We conversed only briefly, but I became acutely aware this was a woman who was very keen and alert. She still looked trim and sporty in her sweats with a voice clear and concise. Seeing her diligence and stamina, I was uplifted and filled with awe. Wow! What an inspiration she was.

Since that encounter, I have used that vision to inspire me to do my exercises or go for that walk even if I don't feel up to it. It's remarkable how we humans can motivate and inspire one another when we are totally oblivious of the power of our actions.

Without a doubt, that elderly woman has passed into her greater glory, never knowing how she, in that moment, affected and inspired me for the rest of my life. I may not be able to recognize someone I met last year or a few months ago, but I have a sense that if I had the opportunity, I could recognize that dedicated woman who inspired me over sixty years ago. She made a lasting impression.

More recently, I attended a NA (Narcotics Anonymous) meeting accompanying someone who was being challenged by their addiction. It was my first of this kind and I was blown away by the beautiful young lady who candidly spoke about her own addiction. If there is such a thing as a preview for bearing your soul prior to your entry into heaven, this was it.

This courageous woman left no stone unturned and verbally stripped herself naked before us. Utterly fearless, her raw honesty was palpable; not caring if anyone was there to judge, criticize or condemn her. The inspiration she manifested was so alive and fresh, you could almost taste it. Afterward, I lingered to hug and thank her for sharing her incredible story. My heart was touched so deeply by her bravery that I knew I would use her story to inspire me for a very long time.

Often upon awakening, as I make my daily pledge to make this a day that counts for good, something she nonchalantly shared, "I remember my MEDS, Meeting, Exercise, Diet and Spirit; this is what keeps me on track." While I do not regularly attend meetings, I do drop in for a refresher periodically and I am always touched by the speakers. This young lady's MEDS message reminds me of the importance to do my own exercise, make good choices regarding my diet and as always allow spirit to guide my daily path. These meetings are going on all over the world and open to all.

I highly encourage everyone to drop in and be inspired by these brave people who are wrestling with their unseen demons, causing them illness and addiction. It is beyond inspiring to listen as they share their victories.

I must give credit where it is due. It was the image of the beautiful daffodils that inspired me to recall these events and include them in my memoirs. Inspiration has the power to cause my thoughts to tumble like young gymnasts, gently bumping into one another jogging loose those old memories and allowing them to be retrieved and enjoyed all over again. That's why I find it easy to say Aaah!!

Sweet Inspiration.

Chapter 21

Guided Meditation: Kindness

To prepare yourself for this meditation please read through its entirety. Then sit quietly and pay close attention to your breath. Begin to read again slowly following the guidance.

Closing my eyes and taking three long deep breaths,

I envision my Sacred Heart filling with dancing pink angels, all holding hands and rejoicing.

For today I have chosen to perform

Random acts of Kindness.

Every time I perform an act of kindness, my

Sacred Heart

lights up and glows letting me know I am fulfilling today's purpose.

I pause and watch the angels dancing as I breathe three long deep breaths through my glowing Sacred Heart,

knowing it is my breath that provides the life force for their movement.

'Goodness and Mercy will follow me all the days of my life." (23rd Psalm)

229

These are the words that float melodiously into my heart, like music notes and lyrics from the

Angelic Choir.

There is an acute awareness that the more kindness I live and give this day, the more kindness will be flowing to me.

I can taste the sweetness of kindness as if it is pink spun cotton candy.

My inner child feels nurtured and fed.

I open my eyes ready to face the day filled with

Kindness

Memoir: I AM Kindness

"You are the kindest person I have ever met." In disbelief, I listened as I helped my now frail and feeble Dad into bed. Could my ears be hearing these words coming out of the mouth of this man who I don't ever remember having paid me a compliment?

Kneeling quietly beside his bed we performed our nightly ritual of saying the "Our Father Prayer." Here I was at fifty-three years of age, on my knees, shaken to my core by my Father uttering those nine powerful words. They took my breath away!

I had spent a lifetime of prayer on his behalf, ever since that memorable day at age of four years, when I had witnessed him being taken away by ambulance, having no idea where, and thinking, my daddy is never coming back. (I had many years later learned that my Dad had tried to take his life.)

But imagine this! My Dad had just told me that I "was the kindest person he had ever met." It was like I was being handed a certificate of completion for those many years of forbearance on his behalf. Of course, I for sure knew this was not true, but hearing it from him felt pretty amazing at the moment.

Instantly, however, I had vivid memories of my precious Mother holding my father's head as he was heaving his guts out after having alcohol poisoning on many occasions. Mother's kindness ranked way above whatever kindness I was offering Dad in the final days of his lifetime.

Still, hearing those words from his lips touched my heart in a way that immediately healed many of the deep wounds

231

experienced over the course of my childhood.

A big part of my philosophy is "it takes one to know one." In other words, Dad did have much kindness in his heart; he just allowed so much of his goodness to be overshadowed by his disease of alcoholism. Just knowing that Dad had found the ability to give someone else a compliment and recognize another's goodness was such an uplifting thought. It was way beyond my expectations.

In spite of Dad's alcoholism, he was one of the hardest workers you could ever meet. He had been a construction laborer most of his life. His work ethic was, "put in a good day's work if you are being paid." As an example, he was always one of the first to get a job from the Union Hall.

For those times, he made very good wages and was always willing to work overtime. It's just that he was like a kid in a candy store on payday and considered what he had earned was his to spend. His bar bill being paid was his top priority. If we happened to be with him at the corner tavern on payday, he would treat us to a soda and perhaps a bag of chips. To Dad, this was his way of bonding and felt he had done his duty as a father. It was Mom who carried the main financial burden of support for our family.

On many occasions I had been witness to Dad's kindness to someone in need. He often gave away that which was needed to support his own family. In my observations, his generosity was quite convoluted. You can be sure; Dad was often generous with his time for his friends. He would help one of his buddies (Mom called them cronies) to build something or to pour cement or whatever they needed. In return, they would reciprocate by

232

paying one another in cold alcoholic drinks as they completed their jobs. It was rare for Dad to find time to repair anything around our house.

He surprised us all in the 1960's when Dad lived with Bill and me after we moved into our first home, he hand dug our front pathway, mixed and poured the cement for a long stairway to our front door and built planters surrounding the entire side and front of our home with cement stones he himself had hand formed.

That was my Dad! He was such a dichotomy of personalities. He could and would perform acts of kindness over and above most men's capabilities. He often worked tirelessly in the blazing hot sun that bleached his hair a golden blonde and scorched him till he was brown as a bear. I'm sure it was his boyish smile and striking good looks that captured my Mom's heart and caused her to endure his alcoholic abuse for the twenty-nine years of their marriage.

As Dad grew older, (I can't say matured) there was nothing he would not do for Bill and me, or anyone else who asked for his help. Sadly, along with all this kindness, he had inherited his father's dark inner shadow of "Mr. Hyde", Dr. Jekyl's tormenting nemesis.

His obvious self-hatred and lack of self- esteem caused him great depression and he often cried and inquired of me, "Now tell me again, why did your mother leave me?" This was at least twenty-five years after their divorce. God Bless him, he just didn't get that it took two to create a stable loving relationship. It was as if he was totally oblivious of the abuse he had imposed on our whole family.

For all his sharp intellect, perhaps no one had ever complimented him on his good qualities as a child and it was beyond my Dad's scope of conscious civility to recognize and compliment anyone else's capabilities. Along with all this, prejudice against any other nationality or race was thoroughly ingrained and incorporated into all his conversations.

His sense of humor was always at another's expense. He pushed every button of tolerance and acceptance within my dearest sister's character. Sis, as she was called, was named after our Mom, Catherine. She was without a doubt, next to Mom, one of the kindest, most loving people in my life. She always gave everyone the benefit of the doubt. She took to heart Mom's admonition, "If you can't say something nice, don't say anything at all." While Sis loved Dad unconditionally, she could not hold her tongue or tolerate his "Archie Bunker" (a sitcom character of the sixties) attitudes. Consequently, they exchanged verbal retorts often.

At times Dad lived with Sis and my brother-in-law Dan. I still marvel at Dan's patience with both Dad and Sis. Sis enjoyed her drinks almost as much as Dad and when they were both "a little under the weather" the sparks would fly.

Between Mom and Sis, it's hard to say for sure which helped most to kindle within me the virtue of kindness. Both ladies were my most treasured role models. Mom only had time to pay attention to her job and her children and excelled at both. She embodied love and kindness in these two areas of her existence as if they were extra appendages. Mom had given up trying to salvage a marriage to a raging alcoholic. For her, it was futile.

It was Sis who fostered the love of animals in our family and brought in a tenderness that I don't believe was fully recognized or appreciated by our family. "Hmmm, for some reason, animals always follow me home." she would say. Consequently, we knew the love of many treasured dogs and cats during our childhood. Thank you, Sis. As the silent observer, I still marvel at your gentle kindness.

Many of the macho men in our family could only seem to see Sis' faults. They thought of her as too high spirited and did not render her the respect I believe she deserved. It seemed to me they mistook her lively, spirited, rebellious nature as someone flawed and missed her wisdom and gigantic heart. "They think I am bad...I am not bad, I am good!" I can still hear her saying while crying.

Sis's salvation was her husband, Dan, who truly loved her unconditionally. However, his undying love for her could not overcome the deep wounds of her childhood. I believe, along with genetics, it was the mistreatment from Daddy and harsh judgment that led to her disease of alcoholism that eventually caused her early death, which broke so many hearts.

It is with a firm commitment that I vow to keep alive her sweet spirit. I carry all the treasured memories of what she taught me close in my heart.

When I think of acts of kindness, so many people in my life come to mind, from relatives, neighbors, and friends to coworkers, clients, teachers and of course over and above all my husband, Bill, as well as our children and grandchildren. Having witnessed so many acts of kindness in my lifetime fills me with much gratitude, which is another topic to be included in that chapter.

For now, suffice it to say, I too have many times, been labeled as "kind" for something I have offered or done. Haven't we all? However, the most treasured kindness was hearing my own Dad's compliment, aimed toward me, "You are the kindest person I have ever met." Wow! I thank my Dad for helping me to accept:

I AM Kindness

My Sis and her
marvelous husband,
Dan (1950)

Sis with Teddy our Chow Dog
~ 1947

She thought her precious Cocker Spaniel, Bootsie,
was the reincarnation of Grandma Liz, who said she would come back to
haunt us. Sis treated this pet with much tender kindness to show Grandma
that love and kindness can heal.

That was my Sis!

237

Chapter 22

Guided Meditation: Grief

To prepare yourself for this meditation please read through its entirety. Then sit quietly and pay close attention to your breath. Begin to read again slowly following the guidance.

Beloved Grief, trying to look directly into your eyes is next to impossible.

I sit here with my eyes closed and try to relax.

My guidance has me take three long slow deep breaths.

I am reluctant to call you forth, even though you have taught me some of my most important lessons.

My preference is to converse with you from a distance.

It is my understanding that my friend Gratitude is also a very close friend of yours. Interestingly, while I am surprised and almost shocked by that closeness, a clearer understanding is coming to me.

Taking three more long deep slow breaths, you begin to come into focus.

Please, if you have a message for me,

238

I am ready to listen.

Grief speaks: "Dearest one, you may have guessed, I do have only one close friend, Gratitude, who accepts me with unconditional love.

She often walks close behind me, anticipating the moment when the shadow of weapons are removed and the wounds and hurts finally heal.

She knows there will be an explosion of her essence at the moment when acceptance, understanding and knowing all come together, overshadowing my presence and revealing the gift within the trauma.

Know that every wound, trauma and hurt has a specific lesson to teach. Look for the teaching moment in all the manifestations of me, Grief.

Without me the world would be in much greater chaos.

I am the emotion that brings about the most lasting changes for mankind.

Sometimes I am sprayed on whole nations in order to awaken the compassion and humanity hiding below the surface of ignorance.

Trust me,

I Am Your Friend!"

With three more long deep breaths, I open my eyes.

I am at peace with my friend, GRIEF

Memoir: I Have Known Grief

In the middle of feeling joyous, the affirmation above may seem ludicrous, but I must tell you, I have made my peace with Grief. Heaven knows I have, like most people my age, had my lion's share of "grief ala mode."

Right off the bat, I want to say thank you, thank you, Grief, for the monumental lessons I have learned. Many lessons, it has been said, can only be learned through Grief.

Where does one start in sharing the litany of events that would be recorded on the left side of my chart under "grievous times" as opposed to "joyous times" on the right? The lessons learned certainly carry more weight but seem to lack the drama that commands attention.

What pops up first is the name Pat Donahue, who has long since left the planet. This woman was one of those classic "pillars of the church." For the most part, everyone looked up to Pat as a leader. If anyone didn't admire her, it was usually because she was one of the most painfully honest and open people you would ever meet. (Hmm, I wonder if she was a Sagittarius like my grandson, Brandon or a Libra like my Mom).

Our family always kids our oldest grandson, Brandon, who was born under the Zodiac sign of Sagittarius, because he can sometimes be "painfully honest." Our Mom, as a Libra, had to always make sure that everything was doled out evenly, always fair.

Back to Pat who had experienced one of the most horrific tragedies regarding her only daughter. She took the deep wound, processed it and used it to help others who were visited by the

240

shadow of our friend Grief. Talk about a living, breathing angel; she was one.

When our daughter Stephanie had her devastating AVM (Arterial, Vascular, Malfunction) at the center of her brain, Pat came to my rescue and shared how she was able to survive the loss of her daughter, Noel. She shared:

"On that dreadful day, after hearing, what is every parent's most dreaded nightmare, that Noel was dead, I ran out into the court in front of our home and screamed to the top of my lungs until I could no longer stand and almost couldn't breathe. The pain was so deep, I wanted to die. I kept screaming until I was totally exhausted. Then I lay there in the middle of the court weeping, sobbing and trying to slither into the asphalt. None of my neighbors came out. Somehow, they knew this was something I had to endure alone. They knew me well and that I needed this space without interruption. It was a wholly "Divine" mystical time.

After I sobbed away the top note of my Grief, crying for at least twenty-four hours, the next day I went to Noel's room and removed all her clothing and belongings and disposed of them. I made my peace with having lost my child and told God I was not going to let this take away all the joy she and I had celebrated together.

Yes, I did have some moments after which Grief tried to creep in and tear me down, but with my deep faith I was able to give her up over and over until each time it got a little easier."

Then she took my hands and said, "Now this is what I want you to do. Pray for a time when you are all alone in the house." My first thought was, *right!* With our three small grandchildren, Stephanie, Bill and I and trying to keep everyone's schedule, that would be a good trick!

She continued, "Go to Stephanie's room, close the windows and I want you to scream as loud as you can until you are so exhausted you have no more voice. I want you to cry and sob and let your nose run until you are totally dry. You have to get rid of all that Grief from all the fluid of your body."

Wow, quite an order! OMG, I knew of Pat and had admired her from afar, but we had never really interacted closely. For her to bare her soul as she did in that moment blew me away. She took the time to come to our home. A first! She came unannounced and not invited. It was as though she came by Divine Intervention. I was home alone, which was rare, and our conversation and soul bearing were the deepest I had been able to get in touch with or to share of my own Grief at that time. We sobbed unashamedly together.

We parted knowing our souls were laid bare and emotions raw. She had appeared suddenly and shared her wound so that I would be saved the burden of Grief that she knew could otherwise take me years to release. Just as suddenly, she was gone. I knew for sure she had come as a missionary of mercy.

To this day, I am not sure if our paths crossed again. For me, it was a time of separation from the church that had played a monumental roll in every stage of my life. However, caring for our daughter and our three grandsons became so all-consuming that at age fifty-four years serving within the church or even allowing the church to serve me became inconceivable.

For a time, I was stoic and seemed to function quite by rote. There was a knowing within that this was a new era for my faith development, and it was time to really grow up and put the tools in my faith toolbox to the test.

We went to counseling, which helped some, but the deep sadness was always one step behind me. I wanted to sob every moment of the day but didn't want to hurt our grandchildren. My thoughts kept going back to: "My precious daughter, my friend, was never coming back to us as she was. How could we all survive this?"

As always, I prayed without ceasing and did finally find the day when I was totally alone in our big five-bedroom home. Following every step Pat had schooled me in, I was able to release a huge chunk of the grief that could have sent me into a tailspin. I thought my eyes and face would be swollen for a week. Surprisingly, letting go of all that Grief allowed me to let go of a lot of toxins and my face and eyes did not swell as they had in the past when I had violently shed tears.

To add insult to injury, my Dad passed away on June 18th, 1991, the very day that Stephanie was operated on, and three weeks later, my Mom died on July 6th, 1991. Neither of them ever knew how seriously ill our precious daughter was.

Losing these three-key people in my life in a three-week span of time hit me like a ton of bricks. However, there were three young grandchildren that needed not only me but the whole family. Our whole family bonded and supported one another as never before.

Our daughter, Sylvia, and our niece by marriage, Judy, and so many other wonderful people were there at the drop of a hat to help clean the house and care for the children during Stephanie's long four months of hospitalization. One of us, Bill

243

or me, visited Stephanie every day, which for quite a time meant a trek to San Francisco and then some time later to John Muir Hospital in Walnut Creek, followed by many months of physical therapy.

Our daughter's AVM became the stepping stone which led me into the holistic field as a massage therapist and a new way of living life. My faith tells me that because of this event, even our grandsons have learned lessons they otherwise would have missed.

A huge chunk of new awareness came when, in Stephanie's words, she accepted her fate and even identified the cause. "Whoa, we've come a long way, baby!"

In my humanness, I used to look back and think, if only there had been a Pat in my life when I chose not to forgive while going through my other grand tragedy as it hit me at age twenty-eight. I'm sure it would not have taken me a full eight years and a nervous breakdown to reach sanity. However, even that painful process had so many teaching moments that help me in my spiritual counseling practice.

It is now clear to see that Gratitude and Grief must be best friends if we are to survive life's lessons. The Gratitude comes so naturally when looking back. We get to see the growth and the new awareness of the privilege of being fully human and fully alive. Thank you, Grief. I'm sure we will meet again, but for now I am content to converse with you at a distance. **I know you well Grief!**

Picture of Bill and Me in 1993
We provided strength for each other as we went
through the crisis of our daughter Stephanie's stroke.

Our four Grandsons
Alexander in front, back left, Shane and Ryan
Big brother Brandon in the back – 1991

Our beautiful daughter Stephanie, 2006

Chapter 23

Guided Meditation: Wisdom

To prepare yourself for this meditation please read through its entirety. Then sit quietly and pay close attention to your breath. Begin to read again slowly following the guidance.

Leaning back into the soft warm cushions, I cross my legs into the lotus position.

Pausing I take three long deep breaths and exhale slowly while I consciously focus on my third eye between my brows where it is said Wisdom resides.

The hum of the air conditioner and occasional footsteps outside the closed door try to capture my attention. Immediately, I address them and inform each:

"This is my quiet time and your sounds will become a part of my meditative interlude."

With my inner voice, I call:

"Wisdom, come and sit with me. I want you to be my friend and have you tell me how to recognize you."

More footsteps approach the closed door and in my mind's eye I imagine it is Wisdom responding as the air conditioner blows

comforting fresh air
across my face.

I pause and take three long deep breaths and exhale slowly.

The cool air assures me that Wisdom has arrived and is as close as my breath.

My heart beating gives me a sense that

Wisdom is speaking:

"I have been waiting for you to acknowledge me. You have acquired much knowledge and experience, which allows me to be present. Many people do not recognize when I have become present. I long to spend time with earth's children conversing and getting to know each one on a more intimate level."

In my mind, I respond:

"I am so sorry I have not communicated with you before now. Ever since the good nuns informed me that I have the ability to one day embody the virtues the Holy Spirit offers as gifts; I have longed to know you. It did surprise me how quickly you came when I called you.

Are you always this readily available?"

Wisdom speaks:

"Yes, because I am Spirit, I am able to be present to all beings simultaneously. If you recall, Jesus told his disciples 'When I leave, I will send my Holy Spirit who will teach you all things.' I know this is difficult for humans to comprehend. Trust me and call on me often.

Our visits will be short since the profound truths will be based on your own experiences and knowledge. You will absorb the

249

message easily.

Your Akashik records are available to me from which I draw upon and will refer to often.

You will come to understand that everything which has occurred in this lifetime has value in assisting you on our Spiritual Path."

I inquire of Wisdom:

"How often may I visit with you?"

The response is:

"As often as you like! Nothing pleases me more than to be of service."

Excitedly, I respond:

"Dear Wisdom, thank you. I look forward to your return."

Wisdom reaches over and gives me a warm hug, just as the air conditioner blows a cool breeze across my face.

With three long deep breaths,

I return to the present and become aware of the footsteps crossing beyond the closed door announcing

Wisdom has left the room!

Memoir: I Am Wisdom

The most profound truth I have had revealed to me by my inner guides is, "Wisdom is like soft, chewy, strawberry-flavored saltwater taffy triple wrapped in black waxed papers." (LOL)! How clever of that rascal Wisdom. She knew for sure I would never have the wherewithal to suspect her hiding place.

However, what Wisdom did not anticipate was somewhere along my life journey my desire for embodying "The Gifts of the Holy Spirit" would shout louder than usual and I would actively begin to pursue my illusive friend Wisdom.   "Seek and ye shall find, knock and the door will be opened," Matthew 7:7-8 has served me well.

Of course, being the trickster that she is, I believe Wisdom was enticing, even pursuing, me way before my quest began to embody her. That challenging, strenuous, spiritual obstacle course that had to be traversed before ascending the mountain where she dwells had to be sought and identified.

Wisdom secretly goaded me on all the way, and she selected a form of sweet (saltwater taffy) that had wickedly bitten me in my early childhood in which to hide.

I remember it so well. Me, at age five or six years, and Mom getting me ready for a trip to the dentist with a painful toothache. Mom issuing a stern admonition, "No taffy! It'll hurt your tooth even more." While her back was turned, I could not resist the call of the luscious pink strawberry, saltwater taffy twisted into a delicate milky white, waxed paper wrapper staring at me from the kitchen table. I'm pretty sure it was calling out, "Eat me! Eat me!" Grandma Liz had bought us children this forbidden bag of treats which we were not to sample "until after supper", per Mom's orders.

Quickly, I grabbed one coveted morsel, unwrapped and popped it into my mouth, bit down and began to allow the soft chewy texture to melt onto my palette. Its syrupy, strawberry sweetness flowed like a heavenly stream of nectar onto my small white teeth and I distinctly remember loudly screaming, "Yeow!" The torrential stream of spiteful sugar found its way into my painful cavity, bit me, and accelerated the torture from a five to a ten on the pain scale. Mom came running as my tears and yells sent out a panic level signal. She encircled me into her loving arms and tried to comfort the excruciating pain.

As my wide-open mouth revealed what had happened, her comforting grip loosened, and her beautiful blue eyes gave me that all knowing look that only my Mother could deliver. I was caught red handed! Mom was not as sympathetic as she might have otherwise been had I not gotten caught pilfering "the forbidden fruit."

Expediently, after arriving at the dentist, the tooth was pulled. You would think that would be the end of it. However, destiny sometimes has other plans for trivial occurrences. From that day on, I had no desire to ever sample (the once luscious taffy). Many other preferences captured my attention and the very thought of that saltwater taffy could conjure up the memories of that painful moment.

I find it funny how a child will somehow take a simple event and mix it all up with tiny little facts to arrive at a scenario that no one else would have had they been witness to the same event. The elements: Grandma's taffy, the milky white waxed wrapper, the pain of the toothache, getting caught red handed, all this served to allow me to use these props to justify my actions. Of course! The logical conclusion is: This was all grandma's fault! You can see that, can't you? Hmmmm!

As my last statement may have implied, Grandma Liz was targeted the "scapegoat" in a long linage of scapegoats in our ancestral backlog of dysfunction. There was a continuous litany of offenses that Grandma chose to live up to: She used to say, "Since I have the name, may as well play the game." I had heard her use this expression on many occasions.

The most blaring of her offenses, that is literally part of the marrow of my bones, is she shot and killed her first husband, my Mother's father, when he was only thirty years of age and Mom was just eighteen months old. While Grandma was incarcerated for a time, with newspaper headlines shouting to the world, she was eventually acquitted with her plea of self-defense.

Not that I doubt this, but her obnoxious actions as the eternal rebel in the face of societal norms continued to rack up a long list of unceasing wounds that my Mother bore and resented from childhood until she left this life. How I wish Mom could have somehow come to terms with the abuse she endured and benefited from the blessings of a forgiving heart.

You might think that due to Grandma's earlier offenses, Mom would have avoided close interactions with the perpetrator, her mother, but not so. Mom was a great proponent of that fourth commandment, "Honor thy Father and thy Mother", even if it was with an unforgiving heart. Consequently, Grandma was an almost constant fixture in our home and at times lived with us

253

for long periods.

Many years before I became acutely aware of all the shenanigans Grandma pulled, I think Mom's resentment came to me via osmosis, the unconscious absorption of facts. It was such a confusing relationship. I believe Mom felt obligated to offer shelter and a semblance of honoring her mother.

At the same time, Grandma seemed "hell bent" on going overboard to try to make up for mom's lost childhood where she was shuffled from relative to relative and exposed to sexual abuse from "live-in" men friends. I suppose these men were supposed to replace the father that had been whisked away in such an untimely catastrophe.

It isn't necessary to list all the facts of Grandma's distasteful life choices. Suffice it to say, by today's standards, Mother would probably have been taken away by child protective services and placed in foster care. Mom, choosing to make the pendulum of "motherhood" swing to the extreme opposite direction from Grandma's modeling, was, I believe, we children's saving grace.

Mom did whatever she could to be the most loving, best Mother you could possibly imagine. She more than succeeded in her mission. Somewhere on her childhood journey, Mom found a role model to replicate.

Aunt Della, to whom she was exceedingly grateful and often referred to her being kind, was apparently a huge influence. I strongly suspect, this aunt became the role model for Mom. While I only recall meeting Aunt Della a couple of times, I do remember one of her children, Joe King, being a frequent visitor to our home. I am eternally grateful for the role Aunt Della played in my Mother's life.

Grandma liked men, boys, anyone or anything masculine. Consequently, our brothers were at the top of her list of favorite grandchildren. Sis and I were treated as second-rate humans by this woman we called "Grandma." Oh, not in front of our Mother, but there were plenty of opportunities with Mom working for her to let us know where we stood on her totem pole.

The hate-filled inflection in her voice, one evening while in her charge as my brother Richard and I were playing marbles on the living room carpet still sends chills coursing down my spine. Grandma, inebriated as usual, turned to her visiting friend, Ernie Shea, and said, "Look how sweet Richard plays, but look at that little rip!" referring to me. I was probably only six or seven years old.

At this young age, what could I have possibly done to provoke such disdain? Having been an extremely sensitive child, I felt the sharp wound of that vicious remark. I wanted to shrivel up and run. Extremely embarrassed, I hoped her friend did not feel the same toward me. I knew that it would have really set Grandma off if I cried. She would have sent me upstairs to the dark scary bedroom that was presided over by her huge black wooden monster we called her chifferobe (I think it was a chiffonier).

I was terrified of this woman and had on many occasions witnessed Grandma's attacks on my sister. Sis was six years older than me and very high spirited. She would not have put up with any of Grandma's abuse. If Sis had witnessed this snide remark aimed at me, she would have defended me. That's why my dear sister was always my hero.

255

This is only one incidence that I am sharing, and I do this to allow you to get a glimpse of the feelings we had toward Grandma. She would turn the switch on her charm and act with kindness toward us in front of our Mother, but as soon as Mom was off the premises and Grandma began her drinking, the barrage of stinging remarks would be directed toward Sis and me.

So, there you have it! Three women, my Mom, Sis and I, all exposed to the "proverbial witchy-woman." Grandma had placed a hot searing stamp on the psyche of each of us just as surely as if she had used a branding iron. Never since have I met anyone quite like her.

Many years later, in reading the psychology of such distasteful behavior, it occurred to me that Grandma must have been exposed to a terrible childhood. My anger toward her began to wane. It is true as Sis and I married and began to raise our own families Grandma mellowed toward us. But the wounds were deep and there was a mistrust that lingered beyond those early years.

Now why am I airing all this dirty laundry to arrive at my destination of embodying Wisdom? To go back to the incident of the "stolen taffy" from my early remembrances: On a day not too long ago, while in a meditative twilight, peaceful mode, I sent my heart on a journey to pursue the virtue of Wisdom, which I had done before.

However, this time, to my surprise, a small black image twisted on each end, about the size of a piece of taffy appeared in my mind's eye. My guidance was to unwrap it, which I did, only to find another black waxy, twisted-on-each-end, piece of paper. opened that as well only to discover a third piece of black waxy twisted paper. Upon opening the third wrapper, there I saw a bright pink piece of strawberry taffy.

I found it amusing, since the vivid vision of my early childhood experience came rushing back into my memory bank. What the heck was this all about, I asked myself? I held the soft piece of taffy in my imagination, which had me transfixed and allowed the sweet strawberry aroma to waif up in my mind's eye to my olfactory nerves. The fresh, pleasing fragrance was riveting. I could almost taste
it's tempting pleasure. Suddenly, gross puzzlement in the form of a ton of questions began to bombard my brain. Was this my mind trying to detract me from my quest? Or, was this a coded message from my objective, to become acquainted with the desired virtue of Wisdom?"

My first question directed me to my long-desired friend, Wisdom: "Why is the taffy wrapped in three black waxy papers? I asked. As I recall, my actual experience was that the taffy was wrapped in a waxed, milky white paper." The answer came quickly.

"You're Mother, Sister and you have each wrapped the memories of your Grandmother in black coverings that have blocked you from seeing the blessing that your Grandmother was in your lives. You have all forgotten the power of forgiveness."

My heart fell and I felt shame engulfing me. Yikes! Yes, all my memories of Grandma were covered in a kind of black cloak. I recall my Mother's words when she shared that Grandma, on her deathbed, had said to her, "Please forgive me for what I put you through, I am sorry." To which Mom said she replied, "It's too late!" Those were the last words Grandma heard from her only daughter. The message from Mom was, "You are not forgiven."

"I will come back and haunt you," Grandma had said to Sis and me on many occasions. Sis and I would joke about this threat, but somewhere in the recesses of our minds and hearts there was an element of fear. Grandma had some very mysterious rituals that we often witnessed but never inquired as to their meanings.

We just chalked it up to her idiosyncrasies. We had also heard from Grandma that she was born with a "veil over her," which she explained "was a sheet of skin." She also implied this gave her some very powerful gifts. We had never heard of such an anomaly, but who knows, skeptical as we were, a seed of her weird beliefs was planted in our young minds.

Inquiring of Wisdom, "What am I supposed to decipher from these symbols?" Again, a quick reply from Wisdom, "You are in a key position to undo the havoc that started many generations ago, even before your Grandmother's birth. These behaviors that have led to vile offenses reaped on your family for the past seven generations that can now be atoned for by you.

It's time to acknowledge the criticism, judgment and condemnation that has infected the generations for eons. The addictions, affairs, murder, abuse, neglect, dishonesty, deceitfulness, greed and so many more of the deadly sins that have been perpetuated on this side of your genealogy can be wiped away and not visited on your descendant's hereafter. By you acknowledging and owning these offenses and sharing your experience, others may benefit from this Wisdom and recognize the power of forgiveness. 'Judge not that you not be judged' Matthew 7:1-3. In past lifetimes, you were part of the problem

258

and you are now called upon to be a part of the solution."

My reply, "So my understanding is that the three black, waxy wrappers represent Mom's, Sis' and my not being willing to forgive Grandma. They symbolize our blocked ability to see the blessings she brought into our lives. What about the taffy itself?"

Wisdom spoke, "The taffy is representative of your Grandmother. Her true nature is pure sweetness. Prior to her incarnation, she willingly sacrificed herself and became the embodiment of all that your generation found offensive and unacceptable, even to the point of committing murder and neglecting her child, your Mother. She did this to help you, by shocking you into striving to gain Wisdom and Understanding of these offensive life mysteries. Your Mother would never have been the exemplary person she became had it not been for her own mother. Mickey, your Mother, missed a golden opportunity to forgive her mother on her deathbed.

The sheet of skin, which your Grandmother called "the veil," was a sign that she would be protected during this lifetime as she committed the offenses that others condemned her for."

Wow! "But why me," I asked. Wisdom answered, "The timing is right! You are a listener. You have actively pursued a higher path that was revealed to you by the nuns that you found so unloving. They too had a mission and by their actions often turned people away from their higher path because, unbeknownst to them, they were not ready. You did not allow the nun's actions to deter you from your path. You had been deterred in many past lifetimes, but this is the lifetime that you are to continue to grow spiritually. This does not mean that you have 'arrived' it only means that you are on your right path. I emphasize 'your path'

259

because this is not everyone's path. Everyone must find their own path by going within and listening."

I was literally blown away! What more can be said? This information came to me totally out of the blue. Was my imagination making up this bizarre accounting? I had a sense that my friend Wisdom, spoke to me based on the knowledge I had gleaned from seminars, classes, books and teachings. The experiences of which I have been allowed to take part along my life path have without a doubt been considered, especially the program Family Constellations, (a powerful method to reveal underlying patterns and connections to ancestors.)

I am in "Awe and Wonder" of this revelation, which is another of the "Gifts of the Holy Spirit." Drama has never been recognized as one of my characteristics. My preference has always been facts and real-life biographies and autobiographies. Fantasy fiction and mysteries have never been my "cup of tea." Truth is a virtue that I value. So, this encounter, while not my first visit from that inner dimension, was quite unexpected.

My account is offered to those who are inclined to explore their own inner journey. If it seems like something from which you can benefit, perhaps you can find healing for yourself or your family. I believe that many of our ancestor's existence, whatever form that has taken, is affected by our present actions. This is the premise that Family Constellations is based upon.

My advice, if asked for, is to Pursue Wisdom with a passion. The journey and destination may be quite surprising, but oh so rewarding, as it was for me.

I would conclude this writing by saying "I AM WISDOM." Something inside tells me; Wisdom is so complex and deep that this account only scratches the surface of what Wisdom has to offer.

Wisdom is the virtue that becomes encoded on our "Soul DNA", (If there is such a thing.) as in our physical DNA and is carried with us from lifetime to lifetime. This is my belief. You can accept it or dismiss it. Try it on and see if it feels right. That's what I did!

Anyone for a piece of Salt-Water-Taffy?

Picture of Grandma Liz ~ 1955
She left the planet at age 63 years

Sis always said: "Well, at least I lived longer than Grandma."
The largest lesson
of my life was learned through this complicated woman. I think
maybe my Sis had an inkling
that Grandma had more to teach us than what met our human
eyes.
My Sis had the most forgiving heart.

262

Chapter 24

Guided Meditation: Playfulness

To prepare yourself for this meditation please read through its entirety. Then sit quietly and pay close attention to your breath. Begin to read again slowly following the guidance.

With eyes closed, I take three long deep breaths and go into my Sacred Heart

As I entertain the idea that

I Am Playfulness.

The sound of laughter rings in my ears and my little inner child jumps for joy.

Visions of a time of play, whether it was a walk in the park or a ride on a bicycle, causes the juices within me to begin to flow and feed my very senses with a sweetness that is like honey for my soul.

Taking three more long deep breaths,

I envision myself gliding on a swing that carries me high into the branches of a huge apple tree.

Reaching out with my small hand, I grasp
a golden yellow apple.

I will savor this later in the shade of my benevolent friend's leaves,
who is not only providing me with her fruit but extends her
boughs
as I climb her and hide among her abundant foliage.

My heart soars and expands while climbing higher into my tree
world.

Becoming the master of all I survey, I can see for miles.

My innocent child mind makes plans to stay in this tree kingdom
forever.

When I bring my friends here, we will swing and eat apples
and live in the trees and ascend higher and higher as our tree
grows taller and taller.

I love this playfulness.

Pausing for a few moments to enjoy my fantasy,

I take three more long deep breaths.

Opening my eyes, I feel the happiness and joy as it continues to
flow through my body.

I Am Playfulness!

Memoir: I Am Playfulness

Never underestimate the powers that be. I mean, why would a fifty-something-year-old woman suddenly decide to become a clown? Yet this is exactly what this crazy grandma did. Signing up for "Zip the Clown's" school, I spent six weeks learning how to create my clown character "Grandma Minnie."

As Grandma Minnie, I pushed a carriage with a baby clown doll inside representing Shane our youngest grandson and had three clown dolls, strapped to my waist to represent our other three grandsons, Brandon, Alexander and Ryan. Children's birthday parties were part of the agenda where magic tricks and balloon sculptures delighted the kids.

In addition, our grandson Brandon, who was the eldest of the four, became at age eight years the clown "Little Squirt." A trick lapel flower with a tiny hose running to his pocket had a bulb full of water waiting to be squeezed if anyone responded to his invitation to smell his flower. He thought this was the greatest trick of all. In my memory bank, I can still hear his glee-filled laughter as we repeatedly fell for his invite, just to allow him to think he was tricking us.

Eventually, many of our other family members got into the act and we would participate in parades as well. My husband Bill was a hobo clown and our daughter Sylvia was "Romeo" who had half-painted face with a large tear running down one side. We had a blast!

Waving and shaking hands with children, we passed out

candy or small little toys along the parade route. One of my left-over talents from my teens allowed me to hit a paddle ball with one hand while pushing the baby carriage. Sylvia danced as we moved and Bill loved greeting people, while keeping an eye on Little Squirt.

This was truly a time of playfulness. What most people are probably not aware of is that it takes an enormous amount of time and preparation before and after an event. Getting the paint off your face is a real challenge and then when you remove the wig, it was certainly necessary to shampoo your hair and shower from accumulated perspiration generated from all the energy expended during meeting and greeting. Still, it was a most joyous time.

The only experience that I truly regret from those days was once when returning home from a party, I heard our two-year-old grandson Alexander playing in the living room. Peeking into the front window and calling his name, I sent him lots of love with my eyes. He recognized my voice, but my clown costume gave him a fright to which he screamed bloody murder. I had to rush in and up the stairs to take off my costume and makeup. He wanted nothing to do with me, thereafter, when I was dressed in my clown character, Grandma Minnie. To this day, Alexander, now in his thirties, has a phobia for clowns, which I have come to understand is a very common phobia for many people. So sorry, my precious grandson.

My reason for wanting to share this period of my life is that while in my clown training, we explored the history of clowning. What I discovered is that it is very common for people who had challenging childhoods, (which may have prevented them from

266

having enough playtime), to be drawn to this occupation for a short time.

My clown era was short lived, approximately a one-year period. That time helped me to reflect and become aware that I really did not know how to play. With our mother working full-time, we children had to carry our share of the chores. Of course, this was good training, except for a child that took everything so literally. Mother's often last admonition before leaving for work was, "No playing until your work is done!"

Since we were the neighborhood apartment where there were no parents present during the hot- summer days, it was where we kids all congregated: my Brother Rich's friends and my friends. We all knew that Mom would be home by 4:30 pm. Therefore, by 3:30 pm we all would pitch in and get the house in order.

For me, Mom's message played over and over in my head throughout the day, "No playing until your work is done." Consequently, I was present and participated in the activities, but in the back of my mind, I was anticipating the "getting our work done," which consumed my ability to find the joy I suspect the others were experiencing.

Even if I was not participating in our home playtime and was perhaps at one of my friend's homes, I was totally conscious of the time of day and knew I had to be home to help get the house in order before 4:30 pm. A great deal of the time I was hypervigilant.

On one occasion, I had a group of my seventh or eighth-grade friends to our apartment and we were having a great time. We were laughing outrageously while playing a board game. To

267

my surprise, Dad came home early from work. I greeted him and we continued to laugh and play. From out of one of the other rooms, my Dad burst onto the scene and slapped me across the face, making my ears ring. My friends and I were totally shocked beyond measure. They all left quickly and I just sat there stunned. I don't think I even cried.

My pathetic Father assumed we were having fun at his expense. It was this kind of behavior that kept me on guard. While we did have many joyous moments when Mom was home where we danced, sang and laughed, there was always this undertow lurking in the corners, never knowing what to expect from our unpredictable Father.

That's why I begin this writing with "never under estimate the powers that be." When I chose to attend clown school, there was not a single inkling that this is what I needed; to experience what it is like to play and just act silly. It felt so good, even if totally foreign. I sat on the floor with little children at their parties. We played games and I asked them childish questions like "Did you invite an elephant or a giraffe to the party?" To which they would answer, looking puzzled, "No." I would then proceed to do a balloon sculpture of an elephant and a giraffe to their delight.

Watching their little eyes widen with delight, filled my heart with joy. I visited a magic shop regularly and I learned many simple tricks that kept the children mesmerized for a good twenty or thirty minutes before it was time for cake and ice cream. While they enjoyed the treats, I packed up my trunk of tricks and quietly exited.

Eventually, I did learn to play, even though for most of the

268

time while raising our children, Ted, Stephanie and Sylvia, I was still of the mindset that I had to get my work done before I could enjoy play. Thank God for their daddy Bill. He always knew how to play and shared that with our children.

Having grandchildren helped me to play and then by the time our great-grandchildren came, I was more than conditioned. The house cleaning could wait or barely get done. Going to the park with James and Jax and enjoying hot dogs while watching the trains depart at the depot or playing with them in their water pool became the highlight of our week.

In addition, our grandson, Brandon and his wife, Danielle, are avid board game players. When they come to visit, it is the order of the day. We have spent many hours laughing spastically during these sessions.

You really can "teach an old dog new tricks." Even if it takes sixty or seventy years to learn how to play, it was certainly worth the effort. Today, I can say:

I AM PLAYFULNESS

Me, Grandma Minnie ~ 1990

Lil' Squirt
Grandson Brandon, 8 years old

270

Lil' Squirt & Grandpa/Hobo
Grandma Minnie & Lil' Squirt
Can you tell who the "Apple
of our Eyes" was?

Our awesome grandsons always knew how to play
Alexander, Shane, Ryan and Brandon
Scaring us with catsup on their faces
1997

Chapter 25

Guided Meditation: Trust

To prepare yourself for this meditation please read through its entirety. Then sit quietly and pay close attention to your breath. Begin to read again slowly following the guidance.

It matters not what anyone has ever done to me, nor what the media is printing in the morning papers! Today, I will choose to stay in the state of

Trust.

I will not only trust myself, but I will also have faith in the goodness of the whole of mankind.

I pause and take three long deep breaths and focus in my Sacred Heart.

There, I see the sweet essence of my friend, Trust, as though she is a vapor arising from a hot spring.

I inhale the vapors and they cause my whole body to glow with shimmering iridescence of ultraviolet light.

I continue taking long deep breaths and the vapors have the aroma of healing lavender essential oils.

273

The sweet aroma opens my Heart Chakra even wider until it fills my entire chest and then expands out into my aura.

Now my entire body is encapsulated in a cocoon of ultraviolet light.

I pause again for a few deep breaths and just enjoy the luxury of the moment.

Then the message comes:

"Because you have chosen to walk in the state of

Trust,

today you will be protected with the

Ultraviolet Light of

Trust.

Remember to repeat many times throughout the day:

I Am Trust"

Memoir: I Am Trust

Sitting in a group of virtual strangers where we were attempting to help one another make sense out of the predicament we found ourselves trapped within, I listened to each one share their journey. My trust level arose and allowed me to open up as well. This was what some would call an "encounter group" in which people talked about their lives and events leading up to their being committed to a psychiatric facility for their own protection.

Two or three nights prior, I had become delusional. Even I knew I was not making sense but didn't know how to get out of the severe depression I was experiencing. It is clear to me as I look back, what I had done to myself. As a result of my quest for a deeper spiritual experience I began fasting. Not a good idea while in the middle of a deep depression. In my zeal for spiritual enlightenment, after three days without food and very little water, I literally depleted my electrolytes, upset my body's chemical balance and threw my entire physical system out of whack. I began demonstrating "weird" behavior and hallucinating.

Bill, my darling husband, was at his wit's end. He was having to work, had concern for our children and coping with a wife who went from "Super Woman" to not even being able to select what clothes to wear, much less how to boil water. All this in less than the span of seven days.

In Bill's dilemma, he approached a visiting priest, Fr. Watowicz, with me after Mass on Sunday. Barely remembering the conversation, I do recall the priest recommended that I be taken to a psychiatric facility in a nearby city for evaluation.

To backtrack and give some clarification to what lead up to this scenario: A class I was taking at the junior college had assigned a project where I was to write my life experiences, which, for me, was like opening a huge can of stagnant, rancid memories that I had resolved to leave closed and buried, "till death."

At first, I danced around writing about the funny scenes that many Polish jokes are based on. If you are familiar with the "All In The Family" sitcom, Archie Bunker was the epitome of some of our family interactions. Our father could have been Archie's bigoted twin. My Sis once said, "I absolutely will not watch that TV program. It brings back too many shameful memories and reminds me of our real life."

Once I began writing, I discovered events that triggered other occasions that triggered even more sequestered feelings which exposed the tremendous sadness and pain hidden far below the veneer of "Miss Sunshine." It was as though I could no longer avoid the exposure that was inevitable.

Little by little, the deeply buried container within me began to leak and the foul black paste of it oozed over the false perfect painting of my pretend life. A dark sadness penetrated and engulfed me, the fumes of which would not allow me to breathe.

The last thing I had ever wanted to do was revisit all the hurt and pain I had experienced eight years prior when Bill and I had a huge crisis in our marriage. Becoming acutely aware of how thin the shell of the opaque glass cocoon in which I had encased myself was unbearable.

It was all about to be shattered, cutting me deeply by the shards of pride which were of my own making. I had forgotten that, in order to get through that excruciatingly painful time, I had chosen to turn off my feelings. A deep-seated fear broke open, uncovering my conviction that if I gave vent to my pain, I would never be able to stop crying. It all sprang defiantly to the surface.

I am aware, now, that it was not just the pain of that wound that I was denying but all the hurts from early childhood and this event was the final straw. The sadness I felt was unbearable and I had three children, a husband, a home, and, worst of all, the reputation of "strong woman" that I pridefully wanted to protect.

I imagined how disappointed my Mom would be. She had always implied that I was the strong one and that I "had it all together." My pride did not want to allow me to show how vulnerable and fragile I really was. "Pride comes before the fall" Proverbs 16:18

Oh, I had yelled and raged and cried when Bill and I had our crisis, but then I felt ashamed when I couldn't let go of the feelings of betrayal and abandonment. I knew we had to get on with our lives and I also knew that Bill was grievously sorry having made a very bad mistake. He was without a doubt the best husband and father I could have ever hoped for.

The pain, however, in my heart was monumental and probably had more to do with my old feelings of inadequacy from childhood than the actual trauma we had come through together.

It was on the advice of the priest that Bill took me to the psychiatric care facility of Kaiser Hospital after I shared with him that I wanted to end my life.

It is beyond belief as I look back now that I would have even considered exiting from our children who meant the entire world to both Bill and I, but I know it to be true. My depression was swallowing me and I didn't know how to get out of the dark hole I had fallen into.

At the hospital, the dense fog that enveloped me would not allow me to comprehend the instructions that were typed on a sign on the foot of my bed. It clearly stated and I was repeatedly told, "You will be allowed to call your husband one time a day at a specific time, go back and read the sign." Trying to read the sign over and over, and not understanding its meaning, I would make the long trek to the attendant's station to inquire if I could call my husband and would be met with the same statement "You will be allowed……."

My request was consistently denied. Panic and anxiety like I had never experienced filled me with a fear that what I was being told was never going to be understood or accepted. It was a sense of utter helplessness and a feeling of being lost in time.

After several attempts and the attendant continually conveying to me that the instructions are clearly listed on the card at the foot of my bed, I finally gave up trying, laid down on the bed and fell asleep. To my great joy, Bill appeared at the designated visiting time, bearing an apple cobbler he had baked just for me and I attributed it to the miracle I had been praying for.

I had no conscious awareness that I had any power or control over my situation. Hearing words that could not penetrate my understanding transported me back to a stage of infancy. All I could do was let go and try to grasp the directions that were being given.

While I was only hospitalized for five or six days, the growth from that time was monumental. One occasion that stands out was a private session with a psychiatrist. For the first time in my life I was able to tell my whole story to him in depth, with all the pain and disappointments. One time following our session we were in the encounter group which was mentioned at the beginning of this chapter. My psychiatrist revealed something that I had told him in confidence. I was horrified and burst out, "I told you that in confidence, I trusted you!" To which he replied, rather nonchalantly, "Who told you to trust me?" I then blurted out

"I HAVE TO TRUST SOMEBODY!!!"

You may think that last outburst uttered by me of no significance. I must assure you that statement was what made my stay at this facility, monumental.

Hearing myself say "I have to trust somebody" triggered in me the awareness that I had never really trusted anyone. Probably not even my precious Mother, who I loved beyond measure. After all, hadn't she and my Grandmother Liz, tried to abort my birth? I remembered hearing the details of their attempts and how amazed they were that I would not abort, implying that they suspected I must have a very strong spirit.

I was aware that Mom's life with my Father was a "Living Hell" at that time and therefore, I concluded, Mom was justified in not wanting another child. However, on some submerged, psychological level or somewhere in my being their attempts to abort me caused a sense of distrust that became innate. I became acutely aware that this lack of being able to trust was my core issue. I emphatically got it! Trust was one of the primary truths I had come to this planet to heal.

I HAD TO LEARN TO TRUST SOMEBODY!

My lack of Trust had undermined and infiltrated every

relationship I ever had. Witnessing infidelity in all the men in my life, the deep excruciating infidelity within our marriage was exactly what I expected and indeed created. In not trusting anyone, not even my wonderful husband, I got my expectations fulfilled in spades. My inability to trust, almost allowed our crisis to destroy all the dreams Bill and I had built together.

It was that encounter group and that specific psychiatrist that allowed me to see my true self for the very first time. This was the "Pearl of Great Price" spoken of in scripture, Matthew 13:45-46. I began to realize that trust is something I needed to choose to embrace and that I could choose it freely.

The true freedom that Jesus refers to when he says, "When you are free in me, you are free indeed," John 8:36, allowed me to choose Trust and it set me free "indeed." If someone is not trustworthy, that is not my problem. That is their problem. When I don't trust someone, it entraps me and robs me of my freedom. It is up to me to choose if I want to trust them

Jesus Trusted that Judas would make the right choice, even putting his own life in jeopardy. Man, that's trust!

Not trusting causes me to become overly cautious and acutely alert. This is alright in some instances but not a way to live my entire life. This kind of vigilance drains the adrenals and causes anxiety and nervousness. I have a choice.

My recovery from this life event was rapid in that my hospitalization was short lived. Many people had been in that facility for many weeks and had not progressed significantly; therefore, I counted myself fortunate. All of us patients had been advised to get outside and run or walk as often as possible. Taking full advantage of this opportunity, I later discovered exercise allows the body to produce endorphins, a natural antidepressant. Exercise became my lifeline.

Once home, I was able to open my feelings wide and finally told Bill how I had harbored resentment, lacked forgiveness and did not fully trust him. I told him, "I wanted to hurt you as I had been hurt." Can you believe it took me 8 years to admit this truth? In being able to open up and share honestly for the first time in all those years, I slowly began to heal.

"No matter what your choices are in the future, my choice is to make a commitment to trust you implicitly", was my new vow to Bill. Trying to live in a relationship without Trust is exhausting and energy depleting.

While it took me over a year to fully recover and shift my life, my faith began to grow by leaps and bounds. All my early spiritual learning began to take on new meaning. The verse "They will see with new eyes and hear with new ears and come to a new understanding," Matthew 13:16, was like a neon sign turning off and on in my heart.

My hunger for learning what the man, Jesus, had to say about life became insatiable. It may sound rather fundamental, but I was truly having a rebirth. Maybe it was a rediscovering of the person I was supposed to be before I allowed my faith to be quashed.

I made a conscious choice that in all my interactions with anyone, Trust would be my most valued response in all situations. In some instances, this has not been the wisest decision, especially in raising grandchildren. As I look back, there have been times I needed to be a little more attentive and not so permissive and trusting.

281

Until children have earned Trust, it is often wiser to be a little more observant for their own protection. (I eventually learned this lesson the hard way). Another story for sure!

I have a small gift shop that is a part of my Holistic Health Center. It is run on a Trust System. People come in and purchase what we offer and put their payment in an envelope provided. Most of the time the therapists are busy with other clients and no one monitors who pays. There is a sign that informs the customers "Our store is run on an honor system. Please place your payment in the red envelope along with the price tag, Thank You."

At first people are perplexed by this practice. However, the system has worked well for over twenty-five years. While it may seem like an overcompensation from my challenging time, it is a direct response to my choice to Trust. Trusting is one of my most treasured, sacred virtues and I will never allow anyone to take it from me.

I AM TRUST

Chapter 26

Guided Meditation: I Surrender

To prepare yourself for this meditation please read through its entirety. Then sit quietly and pay close attention to your breath. Begin to read again slowly following the guidance.

Sitting here with my eyes closed, heart pounding and every ounce of my being saying NO!

I take three long deep breaths and invite you in.

All my early life instructions have assured me partnering with you would be detrimental to my survival.

Every cell of my brain has rebelled against my ever opening the door to your persistent knock.

Yet, here I Am,
at peace and content with a
knowing that until

I Surrender

to the voice of the spirit within me, I can never allow you to take me beyond the threshold that leads to my spiritual enlightenment.

I take three more long deep breaths

283

In my inner eye, I accept the new garment you offer of shimmering white, soft silk and place it around my shoulders.

Your extended hand guides me out of the portal leading to a much anticipated long path.

I see the lush green foliage inviting me to come forward and embrace the beauty awaiting me.

As I open my eyes, I consciously say aloud:

To you my new friend, the voice of my spirit,

I Surrender

Memoir: I Surrender

Changing one's name is no small accomplishment. It took me seventeen years, from 1979 to 1996, to make it official. From the first nudge to the final *today it will happen,* there was a journey that caused me much conflict and hesitation.

One of the obstacles that loomed larger than life was the fact that my Mom was still on the planet in 1979. She did not make her exit until July of 1991. I knew Mom would never be able to comprehend the reasoning nor the motive behind my decision to no longer be known by the name she had given me.

Changing my birth name would have been taken as a personal rejection, an affront to her very being. Mom had changed so much from the easy going, understanding, accepting, fun-loving, young woman who had raised me to someone who became strongly opinionated, judgmental and critical. By the time she reached the age of seventy-eight years, her "if you can't say something nice, don't say anything at all," former philosophy had vanished. It was no longer her rule of thumb. My sweet Mom had in some instances become bitter.

While my love for Mom never wavered, it was difficult to explain to my children that this was not the Mother I remembered as a child. The beautiful exuberant woman who had exerted a huge influence over the person I wanted to model had regressed into her shadow.

Where did that woman go? I knew the difficulties she had gone through. As an infant, her father was shot and killed by her mother, sexual abuse, abortions as a form of birth control, an

285

alcoholic abusive husband, a divorce, mental breakdown, loss of her identity as the strong take-charge woman, shock treatment, a very difficult menopause, etc. All the years of having to be both mother and father, not knowing at times if she would have enough food or shoes for the four children she adored, had taken a tremendous toll on her.

The many years of not allowing herself to express the fear, loneliness, loss of love for her husband while remaining strong and courageous in the face of all the adversity was, in my opinion, beyond any human being's tolerance. In addition, when Mom had her mental breakdown, she finally had to deal with all the abandonment and sexual abuse issues from her early childhood

She had kept all the shame and pain hidden deep inside. We children had no clue about her childhood reality; she hid it well. When she was finally in a loving marriage relationship with Bill Rich, she let her guard down and the deluge of pain that ensued caused her to be institutionalized.

At that time, the medical field employed shock treatment as a remedy for this deep painful depression that had overtaken her. Facing her darkest secrets and being encouraged to write them on paper by her therapist proved to be her most feared nightmare.

Mom came back to us with a quivering mouth impediment that lasted for the duration of her life. Often as she spoke or tried to chew her food, her jaw would lock open and she would have to use her hands to close her mouth. It was as if her whole being was forcing her to open up and cry out for the help she so desperately needed.

The shames and indignities visited upon her from the very beginning of her childhood were imprisoned inside her until she could no longer hold them captive. The book by Karol K. Truman, "Feelings Buried Alive Never Die" described Mom's life dilemma all too accurately. Her feelings finally broke out much like mistreated prisoners when they can no longer tolerate their pain.

For me to present Mom with one more rejection, such as changing my birth name, could have been devastating. While protecting Mom was a big obstacle to changing my name for the first fifteen years, it still took me another two years to accept it myself.

The name Diamond seem so pretentious and grandiose to me. I had to ask myself, who in the heck calls themselves *Diamond?* Being the youngest child of three other siblings, I had little to say in most situations. Also, Audrey was synonymous with a 1930's cartoon character called "Little Audrey." Add to that frustration, a favorite uncle, Frank, always called me "Peanuts." At my inner core, I felt very small. Graduating to the name Diamond, took quite a stretch of self-image and character transformation. It was almost like a *character assassination* to my given name of Audrey.

In the beginning, when I first had the awareness "that I was okay" and the images of gold and then of a diamond were presented, there was no indication or even a hint there was to be a name change. It was just an affirmation that the book then popular, "I'm Ok, You're OK," by Thomas Harris, was information that allowed me to finally have some self-acceptance. I had devoured that book and internalized it as if it was an oasis in the desert and I had been dehydrated for a very long time.

It wasn't until on many occasions, I had people say things

like, "Oh, you are such a gem or a jewel." Or, a couple of times literally, "You are such a diamond." Now, in my memory bank, in the past there was no recollection of anyone ever saying those kinds of things to me. Once I had my transformation experience, and anyone made statements alluding to my new awareness it sent shivers down my spine. I can, on some occasions recall almost cringing and wanting to object. With my throat feeling dry and wanting to cry, those compliments felt so weird and undeserving.

After leaving the Youth Ministry position, which I loved with every inch of my being and held from 1982 until 1990, there was a period when our immediate family needed my help. Our grandchildren's needs and my Dad's health was waning. Now I finally had time to stay home and think.

I was still in the church in other capacities, but even that was short lived. Our daughter Stephanie at age thirty-one had an AVM (Arterial Vascular Malfunction) which left her severely physically disabled. The prognosis for her was that she would never walk, maybe never talk and certainly never be able to function in any way that she had previously. I just couldn't accept that. It didn't fit into my life picture for our beautiful eldest daughter. Her three precious children ages nine years, three years and eighteen months needed her desperately since she had recently been divorced. Grasping for solutions and since Stephanie was no longer eligible for physical therapy, I chose to get my first massage with the intention of exploring the benefits that it could offer to our daughter.

Next, we had Stephanie get a massage. I inquired of the massage therapist if she thought this therapy would be physically beneficial and perhaps allow her to regain the use of some of her extremities. The answer was, "yes." Within days, I was on the phone searching for the best massage school to get myself trained to become our daughter's personal CMT (Certified Massage Therapist).

Little did I suspect that divine providence was leading me into this new arena which was to become my new career choice for the next 25+ years. (At age eighty-one years, I am still doing massage, with several clients per week).

Massage Therapy led me into the metaphysical field. It was within the Holistic Community that I found total acceptance. A dear friend, Alexis Summerfield, marvelous lady inspired and motivated me to take the leap into this new world. By her very example and fearless vault into unknown territory, she was like an armored warrior forging, enticing and guiding me through doors of opportunity with breathtaking speed.

Once I completed the massage training, all the while using the skills mastered on Stephanie, Alexis introduced me to a lady, Betty Lue Lieber, who wanted to exit her Holistic Center and branch out into another state. She generously offered me her Center and in short order, after meeting another soul-searching seeker, Carol Hansen, we took on the task of running Reunion Center of Light.

What a journey that became! This was 1993. Carol and I expanded the Center rapidly, going from a couple of small rooms and a couple of therapists to a very large Center with thirty-two Holistic Therapists. Carol was the PR person and I kept the "Center Fires Burning." With Carol's journalistic expertise, we published a quarterly magazine, "The Beacon" that went from a few pages to thirty-two, with paid advertising and distributed to over three thousand households. We were on a roll and it was fun!

My own personal journey and struggle with my inner guidance came to a head in 1996 while on a morning walk after meditation. I looked up at a Realtor's sign and saw the name of the agent and it was spelled "Dimond." I believe it was her last name, but the inner voice once again spoke loud and clear. "Today, you will change your name to Diamond." It was a no-nonsense voice and I knew after seventeen years of struggling it was time to surrender.

Arriving home, I shared my experience with my husband Bill and as always, he was supportive and accepting. From that day forward, I began making the transition with the help of my dear friend Alexis who had changed her name from Carole Guerrero to the beautiful Alexis Summerfield. Her mentor advised me to keep the initial A (for Audrey) and choose as my first name A Diamond. Of course, that was just the beginning.

Becoming A Diamond Trammel for family, friends and clients became a challenge of the nth degree. I soon became aware that choosing the "A" Diamond was so much more acceptable for me rather than implying "thee" Diamond. The sir name Trammel means a kind of fisherman's net. So, A Diamond Trammel alluded to my being a specialized kind of net, that is, a net to collect other diamonds. I could live with that and in fact embraced it.

My acute awareness of being a diamond net was especially appropriate during the time I taught massage to students in my school, "A Diamond Holistic Massage Institute." It was so evident that among the over one hundred students I was

290

privileged to train there were certainly more than a few diamonds. Hopefully, the training I offered helped them somewhere along their path to hear that inner voice and **Surrender** to that which they are being called.

Chapter 27

Guided Meditation: Gratitude

To prepare yourself for this meditation please read through its entirety. Then sit quietly and pay close attention to your breath. Begin to read again slowly following the guidance.

This meditation may be enhanced by lighting a candle scented with lavender fragrance or anointing yourself with lavender essential oil.

Of all the virtues, you my dear Gratitude, make me most conscious of the Divine Grace of God.

I visualize you dearest Gratitude, dressed in the royal color of purple

I close my eyes and take three long deep breaths.

The Angel of Gratitude
in her soft, purple silk gown takes me by the hand and guides me
outdoors to a carpet of velvety green grass and beckons me to lay
down.

She gently places a pillow of

Fragrant lavender under my head.

The aroma of lavender fills my entire being, reminding me of the times I have chosen to express

Gratitude

for my many blessings.

I continue to take long deep breaths

While in my mind's eye I see fields of fragrant purple lavender swaying in the breeze.

I am totally enveloped in a sense of appreciation and thankfulness as

Gratitude

covers me with her blanket of royal purple Grace.

For a few moments I choose to rest here and allow all the cells of my body absorb her life-giving essence of

Grace.

Totally satiated with the warmth of this

Divine protective quilt,

I take three more long deep breaths.

Upon opening my eyes, I sense my heart continues to be filled with

Gratitude

293

Memoir: I Am Gratitude

Totally re-energized and full of vitality after just finishing a massage on one of my elderly clients, I am filled with Gratitude! At eighty-one years of age, I look back at some of my relatives who did not even get to enjoy this longevity and had debilitating health challenges in their fifties and sixties. Truly, I feel more than blessed.

Yes, I have put on more than a few pounds that need to be shed, but on most days, I feel pretty spry and look forward to doing massage, energy work (Reiki) and spiritual counseling for my clients.

It is hard to evaluate the benefits I have received from recording my memoirs. This process has been one of the most therapeutic gifts I have experienced.   In addition, coordinating Pathways Health & Peace Center and interacting with the staff is like having the opportunity to create another whole family of marvelous children who have become the most magnificent adults you could imagine.

Yes, yes, yes! I have more than enough reasons to be filled with Gratitude. But really, where do I begin when looking this giant virtue, Gratitude, in the eye? I see, reflected at me the monumental chunks of my life process. Having our daughter Stephanie survive her AVM has been the highlight. This life challenge is at the very top of my list of things for which I am grateful.

Waiting for the surgeon to appear after performing brain

surgery on one of your children is like living in the eye of a tornado, anticipating its landing. Only a parent who has almost lost a child can ever know the terror of facing their worst fear. The relief and sense of Gratitude when you finally hear, "She will make it," automatically triggers a torrential flood of tears of Gratitude.

You can't have lived a full life on this planet while raising children and grandchildren without an array of near misses. Skinned knees to broken bones and car accidents are occasions for triggering those Gratitude sighs. I prayed, "Dear Lord all I ask is to get them raised to adulthood, then they are yours again." Perhaps not verbalizing that statement out loud, it was certainly the motive for many of my prayers during our children's and grandchildren's challenging teen years.

Inevitably, I must go back into my early parochial training and remember some of the stern, though wise, admonitions the nuns passed on liberally, "When you run the dust mop, bless every piece of those dust bunnies and be grateful that you are able to stand and mop. Remember always, there are people who are unable to stand. Some may not even have legs or feet. Many children have no food."

Those austere statements still ring loud and clear on the tape recorder stored in my brain. Little did I know how well those stern rebukes would serve me as I meandered down my life-path. In fact, I have embraced those wise words to the point that whenever performing any pleasurable or distasteful task, I call to mind those who are less fortunate, and it makes everything I do more gratifying. I'm convinced the spirit of the Sisters of Christian Charity is ingrained in the very marrow of my bones. Yes, I did soak up their philosophies like a sponge.

We have all read that in many countries people wait in long lines to get even the most basic needs that we in our country take for granted. This awareness is present in my consciousness each time I visit the supermarket. My heart fills with Gratitude and I often ask myself, "Why am I so blessed to be so privileged?"

I would never even think of leaving a shopping cart in the parking lot but instead replace it where it was found as an act of Gratitude for having such a convenience at my fingertips. Does this make me a Pollyanna? I'm not sure! It just feels right to me and the most natural way of being while I say a prayer of Gratitude as I return the cart.

I mean, didn't the nuns remind us to "pray without ceasing?" Living consciously in the state of Gratitude is the most freeing gift my parochial training has awarded me.

Upon awakening in the morning, my first thirty minutes are spent lifting up all my family, friends, clients and neighbors. It has made the "Communion of Saints" (those presently living and deceased), which was a teaching recalled from my religious training within the Catholic Church, a reality. Starting my days this way has brought those of my family who have left the earth closer to me. It has allowed me to connect with the great-grandparents I never knew since they were gone before my birth. Today, through prayer, they are alive in me

By practicing these habits, I now sense that as Jesus taught, "We don't ever really die." We just transition to another dimension or plain. Yes, eternal life, as promised, is so real I can feel it in my bones. If this is being fanatical or using the "opiate of the masses" as Karl Marx referred to religion, so be it! This kind of belief has dispelled any fears of death or whatever obstacles life may bring. Living a life of joy and expecting a miracle every day has relieved me of the fears of losing one of our children or my husband Bill. For me, the "Circle of Life" is a blessing that we are to embrace as we develop an "attitude of Gratitude."

Of course, in my humanness I would miss and feel sadness upon losing any one of the people who are such an important part of my life. Our fragile connection to those we love cannot be severed easily. However, by conditioning myself to detach and allow each precious connection to dance in the wind and not hold on where it is unhealthy brings comfort.

Intentionally staying in the state of Gratitude for having had the privilege of touching one another's lives gives me a great amount of peace. I love the quote, "Don't weep because it's over. Rejoice that it ever happened."

I would like to pass on a technique that I use daily, called "HeartMath." In the book "Freeze-Frame", by Doc Childre, this technique instructs us to create a picture of a time when we were grateful or happy and hold that picture in our heart. While paying attention to our breath and that picture, scientific studies show that our heart produces a chemical or vibration that neutralizes the damaging cortisol that we produce when we are under stress. You may also want to go to the internet for instruction from Gregg Braden on why and "How to Harmonize the Heart and the Brain":

I highly recommend this practice and often introduce it to my clients. It seems the universe blesses me with opportunities that I would otherwise miss or skim over. The more I live consciously aware of the blessings all around me, the more blessings slip into my field of vision and register a signal. For me, having an attitude of **Gratitude** is the only way to live this life.

Chapter 28

Guided Meditation: Patience

To prepare yourself for this meditation please read through its entirety. Then sit quietly and pay close attention to your breath. Begin to read again slowly following the guidance.

While paying close attention to my breath, I focus on the arising spiral labyrinth in my
Sacred Heart.

My breath follows the winding pathway from the deep center as I patiently and deliberately pace and trace my journey to the higher circles of my inner vision.

I pause on my journey and take three long deep breaths

look back at the progress I have made and pay close attention to the winding spiral before me.

My soul is fed with a kind of manna that is produced by the patient manner in which the labyrinth is walked.

The slower the pace, the more manna my soul is fed.

With three more deep breaths,

I can feel an inner peace enveloping me as I watch this soul food

299

flow from my

Sacred Heart.

It fills first my chest and then the rest of the cells of my body.

The manna has the ability to integrate my body, mind, spirit and emotions.

With three more, long, slow deep breaths,

I get a sense of oneness within my whole being, reminding me that my true path and purpose lay along the path of the labyrinth.

There is a knowing that I will reach my soul's destination because

I Am Patience

Memoir: I Am Patience

"I know Bill will teach me." "Ask Bill!", "Ask Uncle Bill." "Dad, will you teach me?" "Grandpa, will you teach me?" When I was fifteen years of age, my then boyfriend, Bill Trammel, taught me to drive. Eventually, he became the "go to" person when anyone in the family was ready to get behind the wheel.

Everyone from my brother Rich, sister-in-law Pat, on down to nieces, our children and grandchildren. No one else had more patience (or courage) to take on the task. My dearest Bill became my shining example of what patience looks like. There were certainly no role models of this exemplary virtue anywhere in my immediate family.

Not even my Mother, who served as a pattern for so many other desired traits showed the patience that Bill has. Even though Mom was the most understanding and compassionate person when in her zone, we all knew better than to cross her. She could go from totally calm to a raging tiger if she thought you had crossed the line.

The Tamborski Family was more than short on supply of this peace-making characteristic, patience. It was as if we were on the fast track to nowhere. Jogging my memory, it seems my Mom was always in a rush to get something done so that she could go on to the next task. "No, I do not like to look at scenery, I just want to get to where I am going",'" was a memorable remark heard from Mom.

Trying to be both mother and father, supporting us

financially and on every other level, transformed my sweet mother into a kind of "Super Woman." She eventually became a no-nonsense person who always had an agenda.

By contrast, Bill's family had a totally different dynamic. His mother, Teresa, was a stay-at-home mom who took great pride in homemaking and raising her seven children. She had a soft easy-going demeanor. His Dad worked and retired from the railroad as a switchman, which provided adequately for his large brood of six boys and one girl. They were all pretty laid back and just took life as it came.

Bill had a heritage of farm people from Stonefort, Illinois. His Dad and older brothers loved to fish and hunt and would bring their catch home cleaned and ready for the women to prepare for the table.

As I lay beside Bill, listening to the purr of his breathing, a familiar tone after sixty-four years of marriage, I realize it was he who had taught me so many valuable virtues. Virtues that I may not have given him enough credit for. There is no doubt in my mind that, very likely, no one else could have had the patience to allow me to "grow up."

At his age of twenty-two, he had married me, a seventeen-year-old who was quite emotionally immature as a result of the dysfunctional environment I had been raised within. Bill's patience guided me through many a storm that could well up like a tsunami on short notice.

Rage was the norm I had witnessed growing up and that was my go-to emotion when I became angry. There was no in between. I could feel the heat of anger welling up inside me when I was offended and would feel like I was about to explode and usually did. I guess there were enough tranquil times to serve as the norm in our relationship or my darling would not have stuck around.

A time that stands out, which was a turning point for my irrational behavior, was early in our marriage when we had a disagreement and I began my tirade as usual. When it ended, I left the room and I heard Bill sobbing in another room. The sound of his guttural cries was felt in the recesses of my heart. I don't think I had ever heard a man cry like that. My Dad used to cry a lot when he was drunk, but that never touched me the way this did. Dad's tears were more pathetic than sincere.

To know that I had hurt the man I loved so deeply was beyond what I could bare. This was a huge giant leap to a milestone in my maturing. Shamefully, opening the door and approaching Bill all I could do was surround him with my arms and profusely beg his forgiveness for my childish behavior. This was the end of my "ugly fighting."

Old habits die hard, though. It took me many years to get over that sense of rage to which I had been conditioned. Little by little, as I observed Bill's manner of handling disturbing situations, began to get the picture.

Life has a rhythm, I eventually discovered. "Stuff happens" and it is a challenge that allows us to meet life on terms that allow us to grow. Over the many years of raising our children and grandchildren and even having the privilege of taking care of great-grandsons while mommy and daddy worked, the patience and love Bill continues to manifest has had a huge influence on all the family. The children too are pretty mellow, just like Bill:

"Dad, Grandpa, and Paw-Paw."

303

Without getting preachy, I can now accept difficulty and most life challenges with a patience that allows me to step back a moment, take a breath and get a different perspective before proceeding. Thanks to my darling husband's patience, I have learned to respond instead of reacting.

I can now say with a little clearer conscience

I Am Patience

Bill at Grand Canyon ~ 2007

"The Gang" Bill on the top of the pyramid ~ 1942
Younger Brother Galen under Bill on left.
Bottom: Left: Neal Brown,
Jim Bresnan, Bubba Walkinghorse
Picture taken by St. Louis Post Dispatch photographer

Bills' Family ~ The Trammel Clan ~ 1955
Front: Mom, Treca ~ Dad, Joe, Sister, Mary Lamb
Back: Oldest brother, John, Joe, Galen, Harry, Harold & Bill

305

John the Eldest had passed in 1965
Left: in age order: Joe, Harry, Harold, Bill and Galen
This was taken at Mom Trammel's Funeral
They were all sooo good looking

Brandon was home on "Leave" in 2003
Front left: Alexander & Ryan
Back left: Shane, Brandon, Grandpa Bill & Ted

Our Greatgrandsons, James and Jax, 18 months old, 2010

Looking at the preceding pictures brings tears to my eyes for all he love they brought into our lives. Our children, grandchildren nd great-grandchildren are everything that gives our lives neaning!

Chapter 29

Guided Meditation: Honorable

To prepare yourself for this meditation please read through its entirety. Then sit quietly and pay close attention to your breath. Begin to read again slowly following the guidance.

Closing my eyes and taking three long deep breaths, I relax into my Sacred Heart.
I feel peace and tranquility washing over me as I look forward to the vision of this virtue

Honor.

In my deepest imagination I see a figure clothed in cap and gown walking slowly down a winding path. It's as though they just graduated from a long period of posture and right presence training.
Their stature and demeanor are captivating and command my undivided attention.
I take three more long deep breaths and exhale slowly.
Every movement of this figure is flowing and deliberate as though they are filled with
grace and goodness.

308

I wave and our eyes meet. There is a sparkle in their eyes that conveys:

Namaste

(meaning "the divine spark in me recognizes and pays respect to the divine spark in you.")

My heart receives the message and deposits
It in the crevices of my heart.
I continue to watch as the figure gently glides farther into the distance.
I take three more long gentle breaths and open my eyes knowing I have just encountered a truly
Honorable Being.
They have seen me and sent me a silent message of power.
True Power is in empowering others,

Memoir: I Am Honorable

Nothing could have been farther from my intentions than to presume that I have the wisdom to expound on this virtue when I first began these writings. However, in over eighty-one years of consciousness I find myself amid the greatest divide in society I have ever experienced. This compels me to address it now.

Honesty, respectability, worthy of trust, good reputation, having or showing a good sense of right and wrong, integrity, etc. etc., these are all the qualities we have come to expect from our **honorable** leaders.

I am filled with a deep sadness upon finding that these essential attributes are totally absent in the character of the person holding the highest office of our great land, the President of these United States of America.

"All I Really Need To Know I learned In Kindergarten" by Robert Fulghum, says it all. We are here to treat one another with kindness. In addition, even though as an adult I'm aware the legend of George Washington's honesty after having chopped down the cherry tree, isn't necessarily 100% true, the sense of pride it afforded me as a child was immeasurable. The story of his honesty inspired me and gave me a sense of trust and safety in our leaders

As a kindergartner it affirmed the teachings my Mother expounded and demonstrated while giving me a sense of belonging to a greater community because of our common beliefs.

While looking for the positive benefits of this present administration, it brings to the fore: Those of us who are beyond

310

wounded to our depths by the rhetoric broadcast from our present day White House, we are shocked out of our complacency.

We have become absorbed with an intolerance for bullying, misogyny, racism, prejudice and anything that contradicts that "We are all born equal." For me, I now know for sure how an honorable person as contrasted by a dishonorable person, sounds and conducts themselves.

I am a person who looks at a candidate and evaluates their policies and presentation before deciding to vote for them. I am not partisan. I did vote for the previous administration because it projected the epitome of how honorable role models for our country behaved. "When they go low, we go high", the spouse of the then president expounded, when confronted with the totally unacceptable behavior from this then candidate for the presidency.

As insults after insults were directed toward other candidates, even another former First Lady, Barbara Busch, expressed her disbelief that any civil person could be so crass and cruel. This supposedly adult male demeaned and attacked others while this behavior was thrust through our networks.

Most of our country was taken aback and reviled by this immature conduct. Can you imagine our disbelief when on that morning in November of 2017, we discovered this disreputable person had won the election to the highest office of our treasured land?

Canceling my massage appointments that morning, something only a huge catastrophe could cause me to do, felt warranted. I sobbed as if there had been a death in our family. That is precisely how I felt. It mattered not to me that this person had promised to boost our economy, bring about changes to "Make

311

Our Country Great Again." This person's very presence was more offensive than any "pie in the sky" promises he offered.

Shame overcame me like I hadn't felt since as a teenager I became conscious that my family was plagued by alcoholism and all the dysfunction that it implies. I was disappointed that the people of our beloved nation could cast a vote for a person who could be so callous and insensitive to other's feelings. I believed this person to be in every sense of the word, a true bully.

I have lived through many political administrations; many I did not choose to vote for. But always, they presented an honorable representation of what our country stands for. Even those for whom I did vote, often did not accomplish all they had hoped to bring about.

Always there was some progress, even in the middle of unexpected scandals and wars. None that I have witnessed presented a crass and immoral demeanor as belligerently as is evident in this administration. There was definitely a sense that this was a person that had to win at any cost. Honoring another's humanness and presence was not a consideration.

Of course, no one person can please everyone. It's just that in my naivety I did suppose that most everyone agreed that certain behaviors were not acceptable.

Our children and grandchildren are now old enough not to be influenced by this unacceptable behavior. Our great grandchildren and those of their age are my concern. What must these children think of adult choices that have found this person attitudes and words okay enough to make him our country President and our representative to the world?

I know children are listening and watching. As I shared i

the beginning of this chapter, I recall my awareness at a young age, of being so proud on hearing that our first President of The United States of America, George Washington, was honest and honorable. Again, I ask, what must our young children be thinking?

Perhaps this is the lesson in all of this: We are in a new era where we must "stay vigilant" and be involved. We must make choices between what is honorable and what is dishonorable. It's not about what party we belong to, but most of all, what core qualities do we want to embody and broadcast to the world? I believe we must choose the role models for the next generation, accordingly.

To demonstrate just one more time the kind of honorable my Mother demonstrated to us children: After enduring an abusive 29 year marriage, Mother, upon leaving, bought and paid cash for a brand new 1957 Ford Fairlane car and gave it to my Father so that he would be able to get to work. In her divorce papers she asked for only $1.00, which she only agreed to because her lawyer insisted. My Mother, my hero, was beyond honorable.

As I finish this dissertation, I climb off my soapbox and invite another to climb aboard and expound. My mother's words still ring loudly in my heart and in my mind, "Walk your talk and speak your truth." My prayer is: Dear Lord, please teach us all how to be **Honorable**

Chapter 30

Guided Meditation: Love

*To prepare yourself for this meditation please read through its
entirety. Then sit quietly and pay close attention to your breath.
Begin to read again slowly following the guidance.*

With my eyes closed, I take three slow, deep breaths.
Breathing through my heart, I choose to love myself.
I pause and remember
I AM Love.
Focusing in my heart, I see the flickering flame of
light and life within.
Unconditional love is gently flowing through the love channel
of my heart directly behind my spine.
My spinal column fills with this life-giving nectar.
Relaxing, I take three more, long, slow deep breaths.
There is a distinct sensation of my vertebrae filling with this
sweet nectar of love.
The nectar spills over, filling my entire chest cavity.

Then it flows in all directions, upward and downward until all
the cells of my body are bathed in Sweet Love Light.

My heart speaks,

"Dearest love,

You have been with me throughout my
entire existence.

Never has there been a moment you were not present.

All I had to do is ask for you to reveal yourself.

Now I am reminded of my connection to

Divine Source;

that which is pure love. My body responds by healing itself and
releasing anything that has blocked my energy flow of Love."

Today I will remember,

I AM LOVE

I take a long deep breath and open my eyes.

Memoir: I Am Love

In order not to be late, I was rushing from having to search for a parking spot a whole block away. Upon entering, I glanced around the crowded restaurant, feeling relief at seeing the beautiful gray tresses of my dear, dear friend, Jackie. Her noble gesture of standing to greet me allowed us to embrace and affirm our heart connection.

We were the kind of friends that could not be in touch for months or sometimes years and when reconnecting could evaporate all the time between us. It was as if we hadn't missed a beat.

Jackie, smiling effervescently, began bubbling over with why she had wanted to meet and have our much-anticipated luncheon date. Little did I suspect her motive and intention would be the bridge to span the chasm that was preventing me from sharing this long-delayed chapter on Love. For sure, the ability to encapsulate the monumental virtue of love in a few paragraphs seemed too overwhelming and beyond my capability. I had come to the point of deciding to omit that exquisite virtue altogether.

Hard to believe the one virtue that has inspired all my writings was the one that I could not even begin to try to capture in something so brief as one chapter. If I were to try to describe my exasperation in trying to expound on that one word, L O V E which the man, Jesus, stated was the "greatest of all," it would encompass my vision of the entire universe. To even grasp all the implications seemed too colossal.

When facing the giant, Goliath, I imagine this must have been the overwhelming feeling the young shepherd David had.

Even David had the confidence he could accomplish the job at hand. My self-doubt at trying to convey the measure of love that I had been privileged to experience in this lifetime gave me the sense that I was trying to explain an Einstein concept with a third-grade understanding.

The task loomed so large in my brain that it seemed wiser to not even try to tackle it. In fact, writing this chapter was the farthest thought from my mind when confirming our luncheon date on that sunny day in late March 2017.

It was Jackie who had made contact two weeks prior and I almost had to cancel because of the need to share cars with our grandson Shane. This was a time when our daughter Stephanie realized she could no longer drive and needed someone to transport her to and from her job. Our lives suddenly became a little more complicated.

Trying to cram a luncheon date into an already overextended schedule was a luxury. In addition, the target date for my completing these writings was drawing near and the idea of incorporating this topic of love into the finished copy was looming over me like an ominous cloud. There was a deep knowing that to exclude such a vital virtue as love from this writing would have rendered it forever incomplete. Yet I really did not know where to begin.

There we were, Jackie and me, in the middle of our mutual admiration gazes across from one another seated at a very ordinary, four-legged, wooden, rectangular table. Jackie begins our joy-filled, ninety-minute, divine discourse, by stating, "I want you to know how important and influential you have been in my life……" It probably took her just a few minutes to expound and

317

transport me to a place where LOVE was conveyed to me in a way that I believe it has taken me a whole lifetime to get a "grasp on" and "get under."

I say "get under" because love has always been something coming towards or going towards someone else. There has been an abundance beyond measure of that kind of love from and for my husband, parents, family, friends, animals, etc., etc. However, this was a whole new awareness of what love is.

In those few short moments, love became not just a garland of affection but a whole comforting quilt of the most exquisite floral essence that may be another whole dimension of the love which Jesus was trying to explain. It is almost beyond explanation. In fact, I'm not sure it can be explained. That kind of love seemed to me was more than just a feeling. It had components of a "knowing" that seeped deep into my soul, the core of my being.

I found myself interrupting Jackie to convey to her what had just happened to me. I am quite positive Jackie could not have realized what had just taken place. All I could share with her was that what she had just said to me, was the answer to my being able to write this chapter.

It blew me away that this dear friend had made a special attempt to arrange a luncheon with me specifically to relay, face to face, that I had affected her life in a very positive way. Now that's real LOVE and Jackie gave it rather matter-of-factly.

Jackie's words reminded me that love is a decision, which I first discovered when Bill and I were at our Marriage Encounter weekend. That "Love is a decision" definition really hit me like a ton of bricks. Up until that time, love for me was understood as feeling. Either I felt love for someone or something, or I didn't.

The love I felt for Bill, family friends, etc.., was all warm and fuzzy. In some of my relationships with family, I had come to an awareness that I may not like some of their actions or habits, but there was still that undercurrent of love because they were special to me. I had even reconciled my feelings toward Grandma Liz, who in my childish eyes was my arch nemesis.

After Marriage Encounter, my scope for loving became much broader. I began making decisions to love more people coming into my life. The awareness that the more I learned to accept and love myself, the more capacity I had for loving and accepting others. "Love your enemies" always seemed ludicrous to me and now it made sense.

I now understood love as: having compassion and remembering "Lest you walk a mile in their shoes, you can never know their experience." That last sentence became the springboard for all my discernment. Love was no longer just a thought or concept; it became an integral part of my whole being.

Compassion was demonstrated to me over and over by many people in my life. Realizing compassion and love were decisions and intimately tied to one another helped me understand they were not estranged bedfellows.

With just a few sentences Jackie introduced me to a new vibration or dimension of what love is. You may ask, what the heck did she say that sparked such a response? In essence, she shared how much my coming into her life meant to her. Jackie not only observed but was amazed by the progression of my life journey from breakdown to recovery to forging a path of my own destiny.

Wow! My path had inspired and registered on her

awareness scale. Wow! again, I really thought no one was watching! Her words were like a key opening a secret passage leading to what I thought was a dark dungeon; that place where praise and verbal bouquets at one time were not tolerated or received. This was a place where I had stored shame, inadequacies and terror.

Consciously, I knew I had done all the work of cleaning out this storage, but now I was able to see that my hidden repository was not only empty, but the walls had been whitewashed and new shiny slate tile was on the floor.

There wasn't even any dust or residue of those old demonizing thoughts and life patterns in that old space. It was now a place where I could retreat and create new memories. I felt I had moved into a room in an interior mansion. As I wrote this, a giant burst of light was turned on and I remembered Teresa of Avila's book, "Interior Castle." This was Saint Teresa's attempt to explain or give insight into her experience of the seven stages of union with God. She used seven different rooms to find a new awareness of God's presence.

For me, it was "The Seven Gifts of the Holy Spirit" that inspired and held my focus: "Wisdom, Understanding, Counsel, Fortitude, Knowledge, Piety, Awe and Wonder", which Little Audrey, Peanuts, desired to embody. They supplied enough "Grace" to deliver her from her illusion of inadequacy and smallness. I asked for these gifts beginning at age seven or eight years. The Sisters of Christian Charity at St Augustine's, Catholic School told me these gifts were available, "free" to anyone. And, who doesn't like "Free Stuff." "You do not have, because you do not ask", James 4:3

Now that I was no longer fearful of others seeing my true self, I was being offered a new insight into a deeper vibration of love, for which I prayerfully petitioned. Knowing there was so much more growth to anticipate and expect because of what Saint Teresa of Avila shared, offered great hope.

Why the quote "There is no greater love than for a person to lay down their life for their friend." John 15:13, came to me out of the blue is beyond me. However, when Jackie spoke, that is how I felt on hearing that my life had affected someone in a positive way.

What I would say, as another way of interpreting that quote is: "There is also no greater love than for a human being to expose their life with all its defects in the hope that it will help someone else to avoid a disaster."

That's what I hope I may have done. That's the kind of thing that inspires me. When I hear or see someone expose their deepest darkest secrets in order to help someone else grow, my antenna goes up high. That is my definition of real courage and true love. This is exactly why I am writing my memoirs. As I look back and recall the many who have unashamedly lived their truth and shared their journey with me, it was they who inspired, motivated and instilled courage within me to reach out of my dark place to find the light.

It was also those who fed back to me the ways in which they recognized my growth, who affirmed me and encouraged me, who opened new doors as Jackie did on that seemingly average luncheon date. Her casual statements assured me that my spiritual transformation was "out there" for all to see.

Thank you to all who have ever extended their love to me.

321

Thank you especially to you, Jackie, for helping me bring my memoirs to completion. I do know :

I AM LOVE

Jackie Black/Fisher/Nielsen

Me and Jackie Nielsen:
Our 50th Anniversary

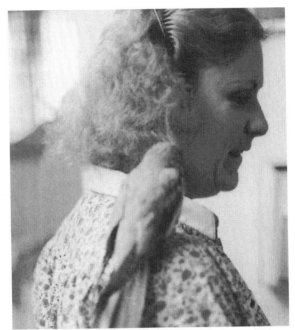

Jackie is a total animal lover, was an
accomplished equestrian and an award
winning ballroom dancer. She excelled in
social work helping others navigate
difficult county services. Whatever she
does she gives it 200%

Conclusion

Anyone reading this memoir cannot possibly receive as much joy as I have received writing it. In the twenty-six plus years as a therapist and the many opportunities of which I have taken advantage, trading as well as paying for therapies, nothing compares with this writing.

Though the many therapies such as massage, hypnotherapy, past life regressions, energy work, spiritual counseling, etc., helped me open doors and come to a new awareness, it was the journaling and meditations that these writings were based on that helped me to discover my true life purpose.

In concluding these stories of my life journey, I have a feeling that this was one of my main life purposes; to get in touch with my core spiritual path and share it openly.

It is, as I have indicated many times, my hope that in writing and revealing my inner thoughts and experiences it will trigger within the reader the urge or motivation to record their own stories. Auto-biographies have always been my favorite reading. Nothing holds me more spellbound than to be given insight into how another thinks and responds to their life experiences.

It is my firm belief that at the core of all beings there is a pure diamond waiting to be revealed and that we have all evolved over many lifetimes from the blackest of coal. Shared in love, peace and joy.

A Diamond Trammel,

"a diamond net"

2019

The Author

A Diamond Trammel is a California State, Certified Massage Therapist, a Reiki Master Teacher, Spiritual Counselor and offers a seven-step program in using the Chakras to bring about clarity of your Life-Path. As the Director of a Holistic Health Center, she has been a leader in the Alternative and Holistic Health Fields for the past twenty-six years.

A Diamond at the age of eighty-one years is an advocate for the "Generation Young" and anti-aging movement. The earliest and most inspiring book, which motivated her to design a program called "Forever Young" was Deepak Chopra's "Ageless Body, Timeless Mind."

A marriage, spanning over six decades has taught her the importance of patience, tolerance, unconditional love and gratitude. Being allowed to assist in the rearing of four grandsons and the early years of assisting in the care of two great-grandsons gives her an appreciation and acceptance of the "Circle of Life."

A Diamond is looking forward to the next chapter of her life-journey; anticipating speaking engagements and the continuance of Spiritual Counseling.

She hopes you will contact her @:

www.fromalumpofcoaltoadiamond.com

Highly Recommended Books

The Wisdom of these authors shined their lights on my path allowing me to arrive at my destination safely.

- *THE BIBLE, King James version*
- *THE ROAD LESS TRAVELED, M. Scott, M.D.*
- *AGELESS BODY, TIMELESS MIND, Deepak Chopra*
- *AWAKENING TO ZERO POINT, Gregg Braden*
- *WALKING BETWEEN THE WORLDS, Gregg Braden*
- *GOD CODE, Gregg Braden*
- *MY MOTHER / MY SELF, Nancy Friday*
- *LOVE WITHOUT END, Glenda Green*
- *YOU CAN HEAL YOUR LIFE, Louise Hay*
- *ONE SPIRIT MEDICINE, Alberto Villoldo*
- *THE LITTLE SOUL AND THE SUN, Neale Donald Walsch*

57197502R00199

Made in the USA
Middletown, DE
28 July 2019